CW00556085

MEISTER ECKHART

Maurice O'Connell Walshe was born in London in 1911 and studied at University College, London, and the Universities of Berlin, Göttingen, Vienna and Freiburg. He taught medieval German language and literature at the Universities of Leeds, Nottingham and London and is the author of *Medieval German Literature: a Survey* and *A Middle High German Reader*. He retired in 1979 as Reader in German and Deputy Director of the Institute of Germanic Studies, University of London, and now lives in St Albans. He has for long been keenly interested in Buddhism, and has also made translations from the Buddhist Scriptures.

IN MEMORIAM
JOSEF QUINT
1898–1976

MEISTER ECKHART

Sermons & Treatises

VOLUME III

WITH THE NEWLY DISCOVERED FRAGMENT OF AN UNKNOWN SERMON

Translated and Edited by
M. O'C. WALSHE

ELEMENT

Shaftesbury, Dorset ● Rockport, Massachusetts
Brisbane, Queensland

© M. O'C. Walshe 1987

First published in Great Britain in 1987 by
Element Books Limited
Longmead, Shaftesbury, Dorset
This edition first published in 1990

Reprinted 1992

First published in the USA in 1992 by
Element Inc.
42 Broadway, Rockport, MA 01966

Published in Australia by
Element Books Ltd for
Jacaranda Wiley Ltd
33 Park Road, Milton, Brisbane, 4064

All rights reserved.
No part of this book may be
reproduced or utilized in any form or by any means,
electronic or mechanical, without permission in
writing from the Publisher.

Cover design by Humphrey Stone
Printed and bound in Great Britain by
Billings Ltd, Hylton Road, Worcester

British Library Cataloguing in Publication Data
Eckhart, *Meister*
[Meister Eckhart, die deutschen Werke.
English] Meister Eckhart.
Vol. 3: Sermons & treatises with the
newly discovered fragment of an unknown
sermon.
I. [Meister Eckhart, die deutschen Werke.
English]   II. Title   III. Walshe, M. O'C.
193   B765.E32E5

Library of Congress data available

ISBN 0–85230–182–1

CONTENTS

PREFACE

This final volume of translations from Meister Eckhart includes the remaining German works, apart from his sermons, which modern scholarship considers genuine: i.e. the early *Talks of Instruction* and the genuine treatises (*The Book of Divine Comfort* with its appendage *The Nobleman*, and *On Detachment*). As before, my translation is based on the Kohlhammer edition by Josef Quint (DW, Vol. V), and it goes without saying that I am once again heavily indebted to him for most of the notes. With this, I have in fact translated all the German texts which have, up to the present, been ascribed to Eckhart with a high degree of certainty. As regards the sermons which formed the matter of Volumes I and II, my original stated intention was to present 'an extended selection' of these. In the event I can claim to have done this and more, since I have provided versions of all the 86 sermons which Quint included in the first three volumes of DW as certainly genuine, together with the additional ones he provisionally included in his 1955 volume of translations for the Hanser Verlag, and one or two others. I now regret that I did not preserve Quint's original numbering for the first 86 of these, since in any case a chronological ordering is impossible. Quint died without being able to publish his Volume IV which was to contain further sermons cautiously regarded by him as 'probably genuine', and I understand, without surprise, that the production of this volume by other hands is fraught with great difficulties. I am, however, reliably informed that Nos 1–4 of the present translation (=Pfeiffer/Evans 1–4), which Quint did not see

vii

fit to include among the 86, are considered genuine by leading scholars. The appended concordances will facilitate comparison with other editions, while the Biblical index will also serve as a guide to Eckhart's favourite texts — perhaps a matter of some interest. In both concordances and index I have corrected a few errors and inconsistencies (in particular as regards the numbering of the Psalms, where I have followed the Authorised Version).

As an appendix to the treatises translated here I have included some matter attesting to what it is now fashionable to call 'Eckhart-reception', namely four delightful (and profound) 'legends' which accrued, among others, round the Master's name, and which Quint appended to his 1955 translation, and finally the 'tailpiece' from Pfeiffer's 1857 edition, which perhaps really does contain the gist of the Master's parting words to his disciples. Since it will probably be some years before any further material becomes available in suitably edited form, I feel that my obligation as a translator is hereby discharged. Perhaps in due course another translator will come forward to present whatever new material later research brings to light. That this is always a real possibility was strikingly illustrated by the fact that as I was about to dispatch this typescript to the publisher, I came across a newly discovered fragment of an unknown sermon of Eckhart's published by Kurt Ruh in the latest number of the *Zeitschrift für deutsches Altertum*. I have been able to include a tentative translation of this as Sermon 98 here. It raises a number of important points which are discussed in the Introduction.

This translation was completed in 1982. Circumstances have unfortunately delayed publication till now. The delay at least allows me to record here *Eckhart's Way* by Richard Woods, O P, Wilmington, Delaware, 1986, an excellent book with good bibliography, which also records the active steps now happily being taken to get the condemnation of 1329 rescinded.

Finally, in concluding my labours I would like to emphasise that my task as translator has been by far the easiest part: it is others who have done the really hard work.

St Albans, January 1987   M. O'C. WALSHE

SELECT BIBLIOGRAPHY

Note: This is primarily intended for the English-speaking reader who knows little or no German. However, some German items have been included. These are either important textual sources or works which can be considered milestones in Eckhart research. The reader who seeks more can now be conveniently referred to Ernst Soudek, *Meister Eckhart* (Sammlung Metzler 120), Stuttgart 1973. A useful bibliography (though marred by too many misprints!), by O'Meara *et al.*, is to be found in *The Thomist* 42 (1978), pp. 313–342.

1845. F.Pfeiffer, *Deutsche Mystiker des 14. Jahrhunderts* I, Leipzig.
1857. F.Pfeiffer, *Deutsche Mystiker des 14. Jahrhunderts* II, *Meister Eckhart*, Leipzig (reprinted Aalen, 1962. The pioneer edition).
1875. A.Jundt, *Histoire du panthéisme populaire au moyen age*, Paris.
1885. H.S.Denifle, O.P., 'Actenstücke zu Meister Eckharts Process', *ZfdA* 29, 259–266.
1886. H.S.Denifle, O.P., 'Meister Eckharts lateinische Schriften und die Grundansschauung seiner Lehre', *ALKM* 2, 417-652 (contains trial documents).
1895. F.Jostes, *Meister Eckhart und seine Jünger. Ungedruckte Texte zur Geschichte der deutschen Mystik*, Fribourg. (82 sermons etc., from a Nürnberg MS; 4 more in Appendix).
1900. H.Delacroix, *Essai sur le mysticisme spéculatif en Allemagne au 14e. siècle*, Paris.
1903. H.Büttner, *Meister Eckharts Schriften und Predigten*, 2 vols., Jena (a very popular if free translation, frequently reprinted).
1909. A.Spamer, 'Zur Überlieferung der Pfeifferschen Eckharttexte', *PBB* 34, 307–420.
1911. Evelyn Underhill, *Mysticism*, London (reprinted (1960).
1912. A.Spamer, *Texte aus der deutschen Mystik des 14. und 15. Jahrhunderts*, Jena. (Latin and German texts from MSS in Berlin, Brussels, Cues, Oxford, &c.)
1919. Ph. Strauch, *Paradisus Anime Intelligentis* (*DTM* 30), Berlin. (From Oxford MS Laud Misc. 479).
1923. A.Daniels, 'Eine lateinische Rechtfertigungsschrift des Meister Eckhart', *BBG*, Heft 5.

1924. C. de B.Evans, *Meister Eckhart by Franz Pfeiffer, Leipzig, 1857. Translation with some Omissions and Additions*, London, Watkins (=Evans I).

1926. Dom C.Butler, *Western Mysticism*, 2nd ed., London.

1926. G.Théry, 'Edition critique des pièces relevantes au procès d'Eckhart', *AHDL* 1, 129–168.

1927. O.Karrer & Herma Piesch, *Meister Eckeharts Rechtfertigungsschrift von Jahre 1326. Einleitung, Übersetzung und Anmerkungen*, Erfurt.

1931. C. de B.Evans, *The Works of Meister Eckhart*, vol. II, London, Watkins.

1932. Josef Quint, *Die Überlieferung der deutschen Predigten Meister Eckeharts*, Bonn. (A fundamental textual study of the sermons in Pfeiffer 1857, with numerous emendations.)

1934–6. *Magistri Eckhardi Opera Latina*, 3 parts, ed. G.Théry, R.Klibansky *et al*., Leipzig (publication stopped for political reasons).

1936ff. *Meister Eckhart. Die deutschen und lateinischen Werke. Herausgegeben im Auftrage der deutschen Forschungsgemeinschaft*, Stuttgart, Kohlhammer. The German works (here referred to as *DW*) ed. Josef Quint, the Latin works (*LW*) by Ernst Benz *et al*. Both portions still in progress. The standard edition. (Note: the *LW* received official support at the expense of the Théry-Klibansky edition, but there is no sign of political influence on the contents).

1941. R.B.Blakney, *Meister Eckhart. A Modern Translation*, New York & London.

1949. J.M.Clark, *The Great German Mystics: Eckhart, Tauler, Suso*, Oxford.

1953. F.C.Happold, *Mysticism. A Study and an Anthology* (Penguin), Harmondsworth.

1955. J.Quint, *Meister Eckhart, Deutsche Predigten und Traktate*, Munich. (A modern German translation. Contains some sermons not in *DW*).

1957. D.T.Suzuki, *Mysticism, Christian and Buddhist*, London.

1957. J.M.Clark, *Meister Eckhart. An Introduction to the Study of his Works with an Anthology of his Sermons*, London.

1957. R.Otto, *Mysticism, East and West*, translated by B.L.Bracey & R.C.Payne, New York. (Compares Eckhart's mysticism and Vedanta) (from 1926 German edition).

1957. R.C.Zaehner, *Mysticism, Sacred and Profane*, Oxford.

1957. R.Petrie, ed., *Late Medieval Mysticism* (Library of Christian Classics 13), London. (A useful anthology with Introductions).

1958. J.M.Clark & J.V.Skinner, *Meister Eckhart, Selected Treatises and Sermons. Translated from German and Latin, with an introduction and Notes*, London.

xi

1958. Jeanne Ancelet-Hustache, *Master Eckhart and the Rhineland Mystics*, translated by Hilda Graef, London.

1960. V.Lossky, *Théologie négative et connaissance de Dieu chez Maître Eckhart*, Paris.

1965. Shizuteru Ueda, *Die Gottesgeburt in der Seele und der Durchbruch zur Gottheit. Die mystische Anthropologie Meister Eckharts und ihre Konfrontation mit der Mystik des Zen-Buddhismus*, Gütersloh.

1966. Hilda Graef, *The Story of Mysticism*, London.

1967. I.Degenhardt, *Studien zum Wandel des Eckhartbildes*, Leiden.

1974. Heribert Fischer, *Meister Eckhart* (Kolleg Philosophie), Freiburg/München.

1974. Armand A.Maurer, CSB, *Meister Eckhart, Parisian Questions and Prologues. Translated with Introduction and Notes*, Toronto.

1977. C.F.Kelley, *Master Eckhart on Divine Knowledge*, New Haven & London.

1978. Reiner Schürmann, OP, *Meister Eckhart, Mystic and Philosopher*, London & Bloomington (Indiana), (originally in French: *Maître Eckhart ou la joie errante*, Paris, 1972).

1980. M.O'C.Walshe, 'Was Meister Eckhart a Heretic? On the 650th anniversary of the Bull *In Agro Dominico*', *London German Studies I*, Institute of Germanic Studies, University of London, 1980, pp. 67–85.

1981. *Meister Eckhart, the Essential Sermons, Commentaries, Treatises and Defense.* Translation and Introduction by Edmund Colledge, O.S.A. and Bernard McGinn, New York and London.

1986. Richard Woods, OP, *Eckhart's Way*, Wilmington, Delaware.

ABBREVIATIONS

AHDL

   Archives d'histoire doctrinale et littéraire du moyen âge, Paris 1926ff.

ALKM

   Archiv für die Litteratur und Kirchengeschichte des Mittelalters Berlin/Freiburg 1885ff.

BBG

   Bäumkers *Beiträge zur Geschichte der Philosophie und Theologie des Mittelalters*, Münster 1891ff.

DTM

   Deutsche Texte des Mittelalters.

DW

   Deutsche Werke = Eckhart's German works in the Kohlhammer edition 1936ff.

Jostes

   Jostes 1895.

Jundt

   Jundt 1875.

LW

   Lateinische Werke = Eckhart's Latin works in the Kohlhammer edition 1936ff.

MHG

   Middle High German

Par.an.

   Strauch 1919.

PBB

   Paul und Braunes *Beiträge zur Geschichte der deutschen Sprache und Literatur*, Halle 1874ff.

Pf

   German sermons in Pfeiffer 1857.

PL

   Migne, *Patrologiae Cursus Completus, Series Latina*, Paris, 1844ff.

Q

   German sermons ed. Quint in *DW* (I, 1–24; II, 25–59; III, 60–86).

QT

   German sermons translated by Quint 1955.

ZfdA

   Zeitschrift für deutsches Altertum, Berlin 1841ff.

INTRODUCTION

As mentioned in Note B to Volume I (p. xliii), the 110 sermons printed in Pfeiffer's 1857 edition are followed by 18 so-called 'treatises' (*Traktate*), of which only three are now considered genuine. These are V *The Book of Divine Comfort*, XVII *The Talks of Instruction*, and IX *On Detachment*.

The earliest of these works is *The Talks of Instruction (Rede der underscheidunge)*, which can be dated between about 1295 and 1298 on the basis of the manuscript heading in which Eckhart is referred to as 'Brother (not yet 'Master') Eckhart', and as 'Vicar of Thuringia and Prior of Erfurt', two offices which by a decision of 1298 were not allowed to be held by the same person. We have here the substance of a series of talks, or perhaps rather 'question-and-answer sessions' given by Eckhart to, presumably, the novices in his charge.[1] The text, in 23 loosely connected sections, was probably put together by Eckhart himself or under his direction. Since these talks, despite one or two more difficult or 'dangerous' passages, do not go into the higher flights of mysticism, it has been thought by some that this was a youthful work, but as Clark points out, Eckhart was nearing the age of forty at the time, and the elementary character of the talks is doubtless due to consideration for his audience. For this very reason the talks may also serve as a useful introduction for the modern reader. The 'collations' of the Latin heading were originally readings from the Church Fathers and the like which were held after supper, being later extended to general instruction sessions. Sermon 55 (Vol. II, p. 75) also appears to be an evening discourse of this nature. The intrusion of real

1

or feigned questions from listeners is found in various sermons (e.g. Nos 2, 3, 4 and 96). In both cases they may be assumed to be stylised versions of typical questions Eckhart had been asked. Thus a prime purpose of these talks must be seen as a clearing-up of difficulties. The basic ground-rules had to be laid out, discussed and understood before Eckhart's pupils were ready for higher things. It should not need stressing that, for Eckhart, the mystic way could only be undertaken on the basis of strict personal discipline.

The contrast with the next work, *The Book of Divine Comfort*, is considerable. This, together with the third work given here, *The Nobleman*, constitutes what Miss Evans (Evans II, p. vi) refers to as 'the "lost" *Book of Benedictus*'. The book was only 'lost' in the sense that it does not appear under this title in Pfeiffer's edition (though the opening text from 2 Cor. 1:3 is sufficient identification), and also because Pfeiffer does not include *The Nobleman*. The title *Benedictus* occurs in the trial documents (cf. Vol. I, Introduction, pp. xxiff.). Thirteen articles were taken from *The Book of Divine Comfort*, and two from *The Nobleman*, in the first list (A) of 49 articles objected to by the Cologne inquisitors, introduced by the words: 'These are the articles extracted from the book which Meister Eckhart sent to the Queen of Hungary, written in German, which book begins *Benedictus Deus et pater domini nostri Jhesu Christi*', although only one of them was condemned in the Bull of 1329 (see note 19 to text). A later source[2] adds the information that the Queen was 'sister of the Dukes of Austria', thus identifying her unequivocally with Agnes (ca. 1280–1364), whose father Albrecht of Habsburg was murdered in 1308. This is almost certainly the event which led to Eckhart's writing to console her, although other dates have been suggested.[3]

If we are right in dating *The Book of Divine Comfort* about 1308, there is considerable irony in its being attacked as heretical by the Cologne inquisitors some 18 years later, since at the time of writing it Eckhart was engaged in reforming the Dominican house in Bohemia where heretical views, as well as general laxness, were rife.[4] It is true, however, that in this work Eckhart touched on some of the deepest mysteries. The difficulty of understanding it is increased by the fact that earlier translators, including Miss Evans and Blakney (though not Clark), had to rely on the poor text of Pfeiffer's edition or that of Strauch (1922) which, being based on the same faulty Basle MS, is little better, and in addition they themselves made mistakes in translation. It is remarkable that Eckhart introduced such difficult matters into a work intended for the consolation of a bereaved high-born lady. It is however clear that she was an intelligent and deeply religious woman, so we may assume that Eckhart's teachings were not entirely lost on her and may, indeed, have contributed to her decision to adopt the religious life.

The Nobleman, which is clearly linked to *The Book of Divine Comfort* as an appendage, is in form a sermon similar to, but longer than many of the sermons in the present collection. Quint plausibly conjectured that its greater length is due to the fact that, unlike other sermons, we have it in the form as written out in full by Eckhart himself. This makes it an especially valuable document even apart from its intrinsic worth.

The last of the four 'treatises' translated here, *On Detachment*, was considered spurious by Adolf Spamer in his study of 1909 (cf. Vol. I, p. xliii), and Quint did not include it in his translation volume of 1955 though, after appearing in a separate edition by Quint's pupil Eduard Schaefer (Bonn 1956), it found an honoured place in Volume V of DW. Its theme is so fundamental and its treatment so typical of Eckhart that one can only wonder, as Clark remarks, that it was neglected for so long. The poor translation by Blakney is not improved by its having been given the misleading and, indeed, rather silly title *On Disinterest*.

Scarcely had the above words been penned, and literally on the very day on which I was preparing to send the completed typescript of this volume to the publisher, when a small but important additional text came to my notice, which I have been able to include here as a fifth item. This is a fragment of an unknown sermon by Eckhart, preserved in a Nürnberg MS of the early 14th century (i.e. written in Eckhart's life-time), which was discovered by Professor Kurt Ruh as long ago as 1967, and accepted by Josef Quint in 1972 as Eckhartian, but which for some reason has only just been published.[5] For convenience of reference (more particularly in the Biblical index) I have numbered it as Sermon 98. Despite its early date the text is not only fragmentary but corrupt, and interpretation is in part somewhat tentative. Quint in fact considered it to be part of a compilation from Eckhart's sermons, while Ruh believes, as I do, that it is part of a single sermon. It thus vividly illustrates some of the difficulties that Eckhart scholars are faced with.

It must be remembered that the sermons in DW, though based on the most painstaking investigation, are in the last analysis only Quint's best guess as to the exact wording. As Clark (*Meister Eckhart*, 1957, pp. 116f.) puts it:

Few, if any, of the German sermons were written down by the author himself or under his supervision [with the possible exception of *The Nobleman*, M.O'C.W.]. They were recorded by members of the congregation during the sermon, or written down from memory afterwards. There are reasons for thinking that some form of shorthand or Tironian notes, or an extremely abbreviated script was used for the purpose. It is known that in those days some persons were able to write down a whole sermon from memory.

Though Eckhart's listeners (at least those in orders) were obviously literate, the habit of memorising, as a survival from pre-literate days, was doubtless much stronger then than it is now. But of course not all listeners were equally capable of such a feat. The present sermon is a poor copy of a bad transcript. It is, however, exceptional, as Kurt Ruh has recently shown.[6] If it were not, as he remarks, a critical edition would not have been possible.

In fact, if we can regard *The Nobleman* as the best possible case of the transmission of an Eckhart sermon, we can place this fragment (ironically the oldest such fragment known) very near the bottom end of the scale, as the worst case, since anything much worse preserved than this would be highly liable not to be recognised as by Eckhart at all. It was painfully written down, perhaps in a Swiss convent as the dialect suggests, by a scribe with little understanding of the theme from a fairly faulty copy made during or after the sermon. The original copy may have been scrawled on wax tablets, which cannot have helped the unfortunate scribe. Yet this fragment contains one magnificent and unmistakably Eckhartian touch, so nearly lost to the world: the idea that God would have burst if He had not been able to pour out all His nature, and that, since no creature could contain it all, He had to beget the Son as a receptacle. One can only wonder how many sermons, and how many gems of this sort, have been irretrievably lost.

Sermon 98, then, though fortunately not typical in its bad transmission, is an instructive case. Josef Quint attempted to establish, as far as possible, a valid canon of Eckhart's German works, using first of all the evidence of the trial documents and other objective criteria to provide a solid core of authenticated material. As he proceeded, he necessarily passed increasingly from the most assured to the more dubious, though with his incomparable knowledge and skill he was able to establish a corpus that will not lightly be overthrown, whatever minor corrections of detail may be made here and there, and whatever additions. Certainly he cannot be accused of lack of caution, and many would say that if anything he went too far in rejecting texts that ought to have been included. He himself intended to publish a fourth volume of sermons that he considered probably genuine, but this was not to be.

The pieces included in Appendix I are in a different category: they are obviously not *by* Eckhart. They are included here, following Quint's example in QT, for their very real intrinsic interest, and above all as living examples of the Master's influence which the authorities might weaken but could not destroy. Their popularity is attested by the fact that all four are found in numerous manuscripts, and they go to show, I think, that there were indeed many who understood at least a great deal of the Master's message. (There are other texts associated with his name, not included here, where such understanding is less apparent.) Who their authors were is of course entirely unknown, though in the case of No. 4 at least we can almost certainly detect the hand of his direct pupils.

The final piece, in Appendix II, belongs again in a slightly different, as we might say mixed, category. Though scarcely an authentic work of Eckhart as it stands, it may well reflect the Master's final words on parting. If so, it illustrates from yet another angle the sort of problems facing Eckhart scholarship. The mass of material contained in Parts II, III and IV of Pfeiffer's edition, together with some of the additional pieces included by Miss Evans in Volume II of her translation, is only a sample of what has passed for Eckhart's writings. Some of it is, or may be, genuine Eckhart, some is 'mosaic' material extracted from his sermons and rearranged, often in a more or less garbled form. Quint indeed believed our No. 98 belonged in this category, but Ruh points out that such 'conglomerates' belong to a later age than the date of this manuscript. Quint may have been wrong in this instance, but his achievement is vast. And it is only fair to state that my predecessor in this task, Miss Evans, showed herself aware of something of the problem and presented material in English guise which was not to be found in Pfeiffer, towards whom she always maintained a critical attitude. She was not equipped with sufficient scholarship, and proceeded on an intuitive basis, and some of her findings were certainly wrong, but her effort must be recognised. In the case of Nos 76, 78 and 84–6 at least, her judgement was confirmed by Quint.

The task facing other scholars, then, following in Quint's footsteps (as Miss Evans could not) is a daunting one. New finds are always possible, as we have just seen. The papal ban made the spreading of the Master's teachings under his own name hazardous, and much of what he undoubtedly wrote was preserved anonymously or under other names. And the very preservation of No. 98 (which long antedates the Bull of 1329) shows how chancy such preservation was: perhaps some of his boldest sermons have been lost because listeners found them incomprehensible or shocking. Anything like a complete 'Eckhart canon' is thus an obvious impossibility, and we must be grateful indeed for what we have, and to present and future scholars who may succeed in adding to the store. We may be grateful, too, that his Church has now adopted a more positive attitude towards him. In a perceptive article, a leading American Dominican, Father Thomas O'Meara, has reviewed modern attitudes to the Master. He writes:

Eckhart's fate in the earlier part of this century coincided with a prevailing narrow interpretation of theological expression joined to a rigid view of the role of the church in doctrinal discussion. Theological developments of recent decades, and especially since Vatican Council II, have freed Eckhart from that destiny of rejection. [7]

And the same writer quotes with approval Thomas Merton and others to show that the interest shown in Eckhart by Japanese Zen Buddhists is reciprocated by modern Catholic admirers of Eckhart. It is a far cry from the days when such apologists were forced, like Otto Karrer, [8] to try to prove the Master to have been a rigid Thomist. And there we must leave the matter. As translator, I have no ambition to add my own interpretation of 'what Eckhart *really* meant' to all the others that have been seen.

INTRODUCTION

Notes

1. It is scarcely necessary now to repeat Clark's statement (Clark-Skinner, p. 31) that the talks were not, in the words of Norah Leeson's pioneer English translation (1917), 'delivered to a Women's Settlement of the Friends of God' (concerning whom see Note B in Vol. I and n. 2 there). Miss Evans's suggestion that the audience consisted of 'probably the inmates of a Beguine House' is also pure conjecture. In fact there is no particular reason to suppose that the talks were addressed to women at all: novice friars seem the obvious audience. If the hearers *were* women they would presumably have been nuns.

2. Johannes Wenck, the intemperate Heidelberg theologian, in a pamphlet attacking both Eckhart and his own contemporary Cardinal Cusanus (cf. Vol. I, p. xxvii), for alleged pantheism, written about 1440 in reply to Cusanus's important work *De docta ignorantia*.

3. The assassination caused a great stir. Albrecht's widow (Agnes's mother) founded a convent at Königsfelden in the Aargau, the scene of the crime, to which Agnes herself retired in 1313 to spend the rest of her long life in prayer. Albrecht was German King and Holy Roman Emperor elect, though not having been crowned by the Pope he never held the imperial title. He was not, of course, King of Hungary. His harsh rule had allegedly provoked the successful revolt of the Forest Cantons of 1291, and his assassin, reviled as 'Parricida' (though he was his victim's nephew, not his son), makes a brief appearance in Schiller's *Wilhelm Tell*, where his base crime is contrasted with Tell's high-minded slaying of Gessler.

The other dates suggested for Eckhart's work are 1305, when Agnes lost a sister-in-law and a beloved niece, and 1313 when her mother died. But 1308, when Eckhart was in Bohemia as Vicar-General and in touch with royal circles, is by far the most probable date. The death of Agnes's husband in 1301 would certainly be too early.

4. This would not be the only irony of Eckhart's career. Pope John XXII, who condemned him, was himself twice accused of heresy (see Vol. I, p. xxvii), and William of Ockham later, from the safety of imperial protection, launched similar attacks on John's successor, Benedict XII, who, as Cardinal Jacques Fournier, had been Eckhart's chief judge.

5. For further details see notes to the text.

6. Kurt Ruh, 'Deutsche Predigtbücher des Mittelalters', *Vestigia Bibliae, Jahrbuch des deutschen Bibel-Archivs Hamburg* 3 (1981), pp. 11–20.

7. 'Meister Eckhart's Destiny', *Spirituality Today* (Chicago), September-December 1978, p. 357. Edmund Colledge (see Bibliography) by contrast strikes a more old-fashioned note.

8. Otto Karrer, *Meister Eckhart. Das System seiner religiösen Lehre*, Munich 1926.

9

I

THE TALKS OF INSTRUCTION

These are the talks of instruction which the Vicar of Thuringia, the Prior of Erfurt, Brother Eckhart OP, delivered to certain of his novices, who asked many questions concerning these talks as they sat together 'in collationibus'.

1. *Of True Obedience*

True and perfect obedience is a virtue to crown all virtues, and no work, however great, can be performed and done without this virtue: and however trifling or paltry a work is, it is more usefully done in true obedience, whether it be reading, or hearing mass, praying, contemplation or whatever you can think of. But take however trifling a task you like, whatever it may be, and it will be made the nobler and better for you by true obedience. Obedience always produces the very best in all things. Yet obedience never hinders or misses anything a man does in any way that proceeds from true obedience, for it misses nothing good. Obedience need never be concerned, for it lacks no good.

Wherever a man in obedience goes out of his own and gives up what is his, in the same moment God must go in there,[1] for when a man wants nothing for himself, God must needs want it equally as if for Himself. So in all things that I do not want for myself, God wants for me. Now see — what does he want for me that I do not want for myself? If I abandon self, He must needs want everything for me that He wants for Himself, neither more nor less, and in the same way as He wants for Himself. And if God did not want this, then by the truth that God is, God would not be just and would not be

11

God, which is His natural being.

In true obedience there should be no trace of 'I want so-and-so', or 'this and that', but a pure going out of your own. And therefore, in the best prayer a man can pray it should not be 'give me this virtue or that habit', or even 'Lord, give me Yourself', or 'eternal life', but 'Lord, give only what You will, and do, O Lord, whatever and however You will in every way'. This surpasses the former as heaven does the earth. And when such a prayer is uttered one has prayed well, having gone right out of self into God in true obedience. And as true obedience should have no 'I want this', so too one should never hear from it 'I don't want', for 'I don't want' is an absolute bane of all obedience. As St Augustine says:[2] 'The true servant of God does not desire to be told or given what he would like to hear or see, for his first and highest care is to hear what pleases God best.'

2. *Of the Most Powerful Prayer and the Highest Activity*

The most powerful prayer, one well-nigh omnipotent to gain all things, and the noblest work of all is that which proceeds from a bare mind. The more bare it is, the more powerful, worthy, useful, praiseworthy and perfect the prayer and the work. A bare mind can do all things. What is a bare mind?

A bare mind is one which is worried by nothing and is tied to nothing, which has not bound its best part to any mode, does not seek its own in anything, that is fully immersed in God's dearest will and gone out of its own. A man can do no work however paltry that does not derive power and strength from this source. We should pray so intently, as if we would have all members and all powers turned to it — eyes, ears, mouth, heart and all the senses; and we should never stop

12

until we find ourselves about to be united with Him whom
we have in mind and are praying to: that is — God.

3. *Of Unresigned People, who are Full of Self-Will*

People say: 'Alas, sir, I wish I stood as well with God or had as
much devotion and were as much at peace with God as
others are, I wish I were like them, or that I were so poor', or:
'I can never manage it unless I am there or there, or do this or
that; I must get away from it all, or go and live in a cell or a
cloister.'

In fact, the reason lies entirely with yourself and with
nothing else. It is self-will, though you may not know it or
believe it: restlessness never arises in you except from
self-will, whether you realise it or not. Though we may think
a man should flee these things or seek those things — places
or people or methods, or company[3] or deeds — this is not the
reason why methods or things hold you back: it is you
yourself *in* the things that prevents you, for you have a wrong
attitude to things.

Therefore start first with yourself, and resign yourself. In
truth, unless you flee first from yourself, then wherever you
flee to, you will find obstacles and restlessness no matter
where it is. If people seek peace in outward things, whether
in places or in methods or in people or in deeds or in
banishment or in poverty or in humiliation, however great or
of whatever kind all this may be, this is all in vain and brings
them no peace. Those who seek thus seek wrongly; the
further they go the less they find what they are seeking. They
are like a man who has taken a wrong turning: the further he
goes, the more he goes astray. But what should he do? He
should resign *himself* to begin with, and then he has

13

abandoned all things. In truth, if a man gave up a kingdom or the whole world and did not give up self, he would have given up nothing. But if a man gives up himself, then whatever he keeps, wealth, honour or whatever it may be, still he has given up everything.[4]

One saint[5] comments on St Peter's words: "See, Lord, we have left everything" (Matt. 19:27) — and all that he had left was just a net and his boat. This saint says whoever leaves a little of his own free will, he leaves not that alone, but he leaves all that worldly people can get hold of, in fact all that they are able to desire. For he who resigns himself and his own will has left all things as truly as if they were his free possession and at his absolute disposal. For that which you don't *want* to desire, you have handed over and resigned for God's sake. That is why our Lord said: "Blessed are the poor in spirit" (Matt. 5:3), that is, in *will*. And none should doubt this, for if there were any better way our Lord would have declared it, just as he said: "If any one would follow me, he must first deny himself" (Matt. 16:24). It all depends on that. Observe yourself, and wherever you find yourself, leave yourself: that is the very best way.

4. *Of the Value of Resignation: What to Do Inwardly and Outwardly*

You must know that no man ever left himself so much in this life, but he could find more to leave. There are few who are truly aware of this and who are steadfast in it. It is really an equal exchange and barter: just as much as you go out of all things, just so much, neither more nor less, does God enter in with all that is His — if indeed you go right out of all that is yours. Start with that, and let it cost you all you can afford.

And in that you will find true peace, and nowhere else.

People should not worry so much about what they have to *do*, they should consider rather what they *are*. If people and their ways were good, their deeds would shine brightly. If you are righteous, then your deeds will be righteous. Do not think to place holiness in doing; we should place holiness in being, for it is not the works that sanctify us, but we who should sanctify the works.[6] However holy the deeds may be, they do not sanctify us in the least in so far as they are deeds, but rather, in so far as we are and have being, just so far do we hallow all that we do, whether it be eating, sleeping, waking or anything else. Those in whom being is but slight, whatever deeds they do amount to nothing. Therefore note that all our endeavours should be devoted to *being* good, not caring so much about what we do or what kind of works, but how the ground of our works is.

5. *Observe What Makes the Essence and the Ground Good*

The basis for a man's essence and ground being wholly good, and from which a man's works derive their goodness, is that a man's whole mind shall be entirely turned towards God. Turn all your study to letting God grow great for you, so that all your sincerity and striving is directed towards Him in all that you do or leave undone. In truth, the more you have of this, the better all your works, of whatever kind, will be. Hold fast to God, and He will fasten all goodness to you. If you seek God, you will find God and all goodness. In fact, in such a frame of mind if you stepped on a stone it would be a more godly act than to receive the body of the Lord while more concerned with your own affairs or in a less detached frame of mind. If a man holds fast to God, God and all virtues

15

cleave to him. And what before you sought, now seeks you; what before you pursued, now pursues you; and what before you fled, now flees you. And so, if a man cleaves fast to God, all that is divine cleaves to him and all that is alien and remote from God flees him.

6. *On Detachment and on Possessing God*

I was asked: 'Some people shun all company and always want to be alone, their peace depends on it, and on being in church. Was that the best thing?' And I said 'No!' Now see why. He who is in a right state, is always in a right state wherever he is, and with everybody. But if a man is in a wrong state, he is so everywhere and with anybody. But if a man is in a right state, in truth he has God with him. Now if a man truly has God with him, God is with him everywhere, in the street or among people just as much as in church or in the desert or in a cell. If he possesses God truly and solely, such a man cannot be disturbed by anybody. Why?

He has only God, thinks only of God, and all things are for him nothing but God. Such a man bears God in all his works and everywhere, and all that man's works are wrought purely by God — for he who causes the work is more genuinely and truly the owner of the work than he who performs it. If we then have none but God alone in mind, then He must really do our work, and God's work can be hindered by none, nor by any company or place. Therefore no one can stop such a man, for he regards, seeks and tastes nothing but God, for God is united with that man in all his aims. And just as no multiplicity can scatter God, so nothing can scatter or diversify that man, for he is one in the One, where all multiplicity is one and is non-multiplicity.

16

A man should receive God in all things and train his mind to keep God ever present in his mind, in his aims and in his love. Note how you regard God: keep the same attitude that you have in church or in your cell, and carry it with you in the crowd and in unrest and inequality.[7] And — as I have often said — when we speak of 'equality', this does not mean that one should regard all works as equal, or all places or people. That would be quite wrong, for praying is a better task than spinning, and the church is a nobler place than the street. But in your acts you should have an equal mind and equal faith and equal love for your God, and equal seriousness. Assuredly, if you were equal-minded in this way, then no man could keep you from having God ever present.

But if God is not thus truly in a man, but has to be got from without, from this and that, if he seeks God in unequal fashion, whether in deeds or in people or in places, that man has not got God. And that man may easily be distracted, since he has not got God, and does not seek God alone, or love and strive for God alone. Accordingly he is put off not only by *bad* company — even goodness is a hindrance to him: not only the street but even the church, and not only evil words and deeds but even good words and deeds, for the blockage is within himself because in him God has not become all things. If this were so, then he would be happy and at ease everywhere and with everybody, for he would have God, whom none can take from him, nor could anyone hinder his work.

Wherein lies this true possession of God — this *really* having Him? This true possession of God depends on the mind, an inner mental turning and striving towards God — but not in a continuous and equal thinking of Him, for that

17

would be impossible for nature to strive for, very difficult and not even the best thing. A man should not have, or be satisfied with, an imagined God, for then, when the idea vanishes, God vanishes! Rather, one should have an essential God, who far transcends the thought of man and all creatures. Such a God never vanishes unless a man wilfully turns away from Him.

He who has God thus essentially, takes Him divinely, and for him God shines forth in all things, for all things taste divinely to him, and God's image appears to him from out of all things. God flashes forth in him always, in him there is detachment and turning away, and he bears the imprint of his beloved, present God. It is just like a man who is terribly thirsty: he can do other things beside drinking and can even turn his mind to other thoughts, but yet, whatever he does and in whatever company he is, whatever he intends, whatever he thinks or does, he never loses the thought of drinking as long as his thirst lasts; and the greater the thirst, the greater and deeper and more present and persistent will be the thought of a drink. Or if there is a man who is so passionately devoted to a thing that nothing else interests him or touches his heart, he is intent on that thing and nothing else; quite certainly, wherever or with whomever that man is, and whatever he takes up or does, the image of what he loves never fades in him, and he finds its image in everything, and it is ever the more strongly present to him, the more his love for it increases. And that man will not seek rest, for no unrest disturbs him.

That man finds greater praise before God, for he takes all things as divine, and as greater than they are in themselves. Indeed, this requires zeal and love and a clear perception of the interior life, and a watchful, true, wise and real knowledge of what the mind is occupied with among things and people. *This* cannot be learnt by running away, by fleeing into the desert away from outward things; a man must learn to acquire an inward desert, wherever and with whomever he is. He must learn to break through things and seize his God in them, and to make His image grow in himself in essential wise. It is just like learning to write: truly, if a man is to acquire this art, he must apply himself and practise hard, however heavy and bitter a task it seems to him, and however impossible. If he is prepared to practise diligently and often, he will learn and master the art. Of course, at first he has to remember every letter and fix it firmly in his mind. Later on, when he has acquired the art, he will be completely free of the image and will not have to stop and think, but will write fluently and freely — and the same with playing the fiddle or any other task that requires skill. All he needs to know is that he intends to exercise his skill, and even if he is not paying full attention, wherever his thoughts may stray, he will do the job because he has the skill. Thus a man should be pervaded with God's presence, transformed with the form of his beloved God, and made essential by Him, so that God's presence shines for him without any effort; rather he will find emptiness in all things and be totally free of things. But first there must be thought and attentive study, just as with a pupil in any art.

7. *How to Perform One's Work in the Most Rational Way*
We find many people at the stage — which a man can easily reach if he will — where the things a man moves among do not hinder him or leave any lasting image with him: for when

the heart is full of God, creatures cannot have or find a place in it. But this is not enough: we should gain more profit from all things, whatever they may be, wherever we are, whatever we see or hear, and however strange or alien it may be. Only then are we in a right state and not before, and a man can never come to an end of this, but can continue to grow and gain more and more in genuine increase. And in all his acts and in all things a man should consciously use his reason, having in all things a perceptive awareness of himself and his inward being, and in all things seize God in the highest possible way. For a man should be as our Lord said, "Like people on the watch, always expecting their Lord" (Luke 12:36). For indeed, people who are expectant like that are watchful, they look around them to see where he whom they expect is coming from, and they look out for him in whatever comes along, however strange it may be, just in case he should be in it. In this way we should consciously discover our Lord in all things. This requires much diligence, demanding a total effort of our senses and powers of mind; then those who manage this are in a right state: taking God equally in all things, they find God in equal measure in all.

It is true that one piece of work differs from another, but if a man were to do all things with an equal mind, then indeed his works would all be equal, and for a man in a right state, who should thus possess God, God would shine forth as nakedy in the most worldly things as in the most godly. Not of course that a man should do anything worldly or unfitting, but rather: whatever of outward things he should chance to see or hear, he should turn to God. He to whom God is thus present in all things, who is in full control of his reason and uses it, he alone knows true peace, and he has heaven indeed.

For him who would be in a right state, one of two things must happen: either he must seize God in activities, and learn to have Him, or he must abandon all works. But since man cannot in this life refrain from activities, which are human and manifold, so a man should learn to have his God in all things and remain unhindered in all acts and places. And so, when a beginner has to deal with people, he should first arm himself strongly with God and fix Him firmly in his heart, uniting all his intentions, thoughts, will and strength with Him, so that nothing else can arise in that man's mind.

8. *On Unremitting Effort in the Highest Progress*

A man should never regard a task so easily and as so well done, that he becomes too free in his actions or so confident as to let his reason become idle and go to sleep. He should always lift himself up with the twin powers of reason and will, seizing his highest good therein at their peak, and wisely guarding himself against all harm, both outwardly and inwardly. In this way he will never fail in anything, but will continue to make great progress.

9. *How the Inclination to Sin is Always Salutary to Man*

You should know that the impulse to wrong-doing is not without great benefit and use to the righteous. Now see: here are two men; one of them is such that he is subject to no weaknesses, or hardly any; while the other is one who is subject to temptations. By the outward presence of things his outer man is moved, maybe to anger or to vanity or perhaps to sensuality, according to whatever object he encounters. But with his highest powers he stands firm, unmoved, and will not yield to temptation, whether it be anger or any sin, and thus he fights strongly against temptation, for the weakness may well be a part of his nature, just as many a man is by nature angry or proud or whatever it may be, but still he will not sin. This one deserves far more praise, his reward is much greater and his virtue nobler than that of the first man, for perfection of virtue comes by struggle. As St Paul says: "Virtue is perfected in weakness" (2 Cor. 12:9).

Inclination to sin is not sin, but willingness to sin is sin, willingness to be angry is sin. Truly, if a man who was in a right state had the power to wish, he would not wish to lose his inclination to sin, for without this a man would be uncertain in all things and in all his acts, without a care for things, and would also miss the honour of struggle, victory and reward; for the temptation and the stimulus of vice bring forth virtue and the reward of effort. For this inclination makes a man ever more zealous to practise virtue strongly, it drives him by force to virtue and is a sharp lash which compels a man to mindfulness and virtue, for the weaker a man finds himself to be, the more he should arm himself with strength and victory. For virtue and vice both depend on the will.

10. *How the Will Can Do All Things, and How All Virtues Rest in the Will, Provided Only that it is Just*

A man should not be too greatly frightened of anything as long as he knows himself to be of good will, and he should not be too sad if he cannot carry out his intentions. But he should not think himself far from all virtues if he is aware of a good will in himself, for virtue and all goodness lies in a good will. If you have a true and proper will, you can lack nothing, neither love nor humility nor any other virtue. But what you will strongly and with all your will, that you *have*, and neither God nor all creatures can take it from you if your will is perfect and a true godly will, and *in the present*. Not 'I want later on', but 'I will that it shall be so *now*!' If a thing were a thousand miles aways and I want to have it, it is more truly mine than something in my lap that I don't want.

Good is no less powerful for good than evil is for evil. Note this: though I might never have done an evil deed, yet if I had the will to do evil, the sin is mine, just as if I had done the deed; if I were utterly determined I could commit as great a sin as if I had murdered the whole world without actually doing a thing toward it. Why should not the same be true of a good will? Indeed it is, in fact incomparably more so.

In fact, with the will I can do all things. I can endure the sorrows of all men, feed all the poor and do all men's work, or whatever you can think of. If you have lacked only in the power and not in the will, then in the eyes of God you have done it all, and no one can take this from you or hinder you for a moment, for the will to do as soon as I can is the same in the sight of God as having done the deed. Further, if I wanted to have all the will in the world, and if my desire for this were strong and perfect, then I truly *have* it, for what I will to have, I have. Again, if I truly wanted to have as much love as all men have ever possessed, to praise God as much, or what you will, you truly possess it if your will is entire.

Now you may ask when the will is a right will. The will is perfect and right when it is without all attachment, when it has gone out of self and is shaped and formed after the will of God. The more this is so, the more perfect and true the will. And with *that* will you can do anything, love or anything else.

23

You ask, 'How can I have this love if I don't feel it or notice it, such as I see in many people who perform great deeds, and in whom I see great devotion or wondrous things which I have not got?'

In this connection you should note two things about love: the one is the *essence* of love, the other is the *work* or expression of love. The place of the essence of love is in the will alone: whoever has more will has more love. But as to who has more of this, no man knows concerning another — it lies hidden in the soul as long as God lies hidden in the ground of the soul. This love lies wholly in the will, and whoever has more will has more love. Then there is another thing, the expression and work of love. *That* shines forth as inwardness and devotion and jubilation, and this is not always the best thing; for sometimes it is not from love, but sometimes it comes from nature that one has such savour and sweetness, or it can come from the influence of heaven or borne in by the senses. And those who have more of this are not always the best people, for though it may well come from God, yet our Lord gives it to such folk as an enticement and a stimulus, or as a way of keeping them apart from other people. But when such people later on gain more love, they may not have so much feeling or sensation, and then it clearly appears that they have love, if without such support they remain wholly and steadfastly faithful to God.

But even supposing this is entirely love, it is still not the best thing; that appears in this, that one must sometimes leave such a state of joy for a better one of love, and sometimes to perform a work of love where it is needed, whether it be spiritual or bodily. As I have said before, if a man were in an ecstasy as St Paul was (2 Cor. 12: 2–4), and if he knew of a sick person who needed a bowl of soup from him, I would consider it far better if you were to leave that rapture out of love and help the needy person out of greater love.

A man should not suppose that in this way he is bereft of grace for, whatever a man willingly gives up for love, he shall receive in nobler fashion; as Christ says: "He who leaves anything for my sake will receive again a hundredfold" (Matt. 19:29). Truly, whatever a man gives up or renounces for God's sake, even if that man greatly yearns for the consolation of such feelings and such inwardness, and does all he can to get it, and God denies it to him — if he renounces and does without for God's sake, then in truth he will find it just as if he had been possessed of all goods in fee simple and had willingly left it, renounced it and given it up for God: he will be rewarded a hundredfold. For whatever a man would have, if he renounces and does without for God's sake, whether it is physical or spiritual, he will find it all in God just as if he had had it and had willingly abandoned it; for a man must consent to be deprived of all things for God's sake, and in love he must abandon and do without all comfort for very love.

That one should at times leave such feelings for love we learn from the loving St Paul, who said: "I have wished to be separated from the love of Christ for love of my brothers" (Rom. 9:3). The way he meant it was this — not in the first sense of love, for he would not be separated from that one instant for all that is in heaven and earth, but in the consolation.

However, you should know that God's friends[8] are never without consolation, for whatever God wills is their greatest consolation, whether it is comfort or discomfort.

11. *What a Man Should Do When He Misses God, Who is in Hiding*

You should also know that the good will cannot miss God. But the mind's perceptive faculty sometimes misses Him, and often thinks God has gone away. What should you do then? Do exactly the same as if you were in the greatest comfort; learn to do the same when you are in the greatest distress, and behave just as you behaved then. No counsel is so good for finding God as to seek where you left Him; and if you now do, while you miss Him, just as you did when you last had Him, then you will find Him. But a good will never loses or misses God at any time. Many people say 'We have a good will', but they have not God's will: they want to have *their* will, or they want to teach our Lord to do such and such. That is not good will. We must seek to find God's own dearest will.

God's intent in all things is that we should give up our will. When St Paul spoke a great deal to our Lord, and our Lord to him, this availed him nothing till he abandoned his will and said: "Lord, what do you want me to do?" (Acts 9:6). Then our Lord knew well what he should do. So too, when the angel appeared to our Lady: nothing that she or he said to one another could have made her the mother of God, but as soon as she gave up her will, at once she became a true mother of the eternal Word and conceived God straight away: he became her natural son. Moreover, nothing can make a true man but the giving up of the will. Indeed, except by giving up our will in all things we cannot achieve anything with God. But if it should come to the point that we gave up all of our will, daring to abandon all things for God's sake, *then* we should have done all things, and not before.

26

There are not many people who — whether they know it or not — do not wish to be in such a state and to feel lofty emotions about it, that is, they want to have this condition and the profit together — but this is nothing but self-will. You must give yourself up wholly to God in every respect, not caring what He does with His own. Thousands have died and gone to heaven who never departed perfectly from their own will, but that alone would be a perfect and true will if one had completely entered into God's will and were without a will of one's own. Whoever has more of that is more, and more truly, established in God. Even one *Ave Maria* said in this spirit, when a man has gone out of himself, is of more value than reading a thousand psalters without it. In fact a single step with it would be better than crossing the sea without it.

A man who had thus thoroughly abandoned self and everything pertaining to self would in truth be so firmly established in God that, wherever you touched him you would first touch God, for he is completely in God and God is all round him just as my cowl is round my head, and if anyone wants to take hold of me, he must first touch my clothing. In the same way, if I want to drink, the drink must first pass over my tongue, where it gains its taste. If my tongue is coated with bitterness, then indeed, however sweet the wine may be in itself, it must become bitter by the means through which it reaches me. Truly, a man who had quite renounced his own would be so surrounded by God that all creatures could not touch him, and whatever got to him would have to pass through God, and in doing so take on His flavour and become godlike.

However great the suffering may be, if it comes through

God, then God suffers first from it.[9] Indeed, by the truth that *is* God, there never was so tiny a pang of sorrow that befell a man, not the least little discomfort or inconvenience, but if he placed it in God, then it would pain God incomparably more than that man, and incommode God more than the man himself. But if God endures this for the sake of such benefit as He intends for you thereby, and if *you* will endure that which God endures and which comes to you *through* Him, then it inevitably becomes godlike, so that shame is like honour, bitterness like sweetness and the blackest darkness like the brightest light. It takes all its savour from God and becomes godlike: for whatever comes to such a man conforms to God, because he seeks nothing else and has no taste for anything else. Accordingly, he gets hold of God in all bitterness just as in the greatest sweetness.

The light shines in the darkness, and then we are aware of it. What good is the teaching or the light to people unless they make use of it? When they are in darkness or in sorrow, *then* they will see the light.

The more we are owned, the less we own.[10] A man who should have gone out of himself could never fail of God in any works. But should it happen that such a man slipped or erred in speech, or that something wrong crept in, since God began the work He must bear the damage: therefore you should on no account abandon your work. We find this exemplified in St Bernard and other saints. In this life we can never be quite free from such incidents. Just because tares sometimes grow among the corn, you should not on that account reject the good corn. Truly, for a man in a right state who knows God's ways, such accidents would be of great profit. For to the good, all things work for the good, as St

Paul says (Rom. 8:28), and as St Augustine says, 'Yes, even sins'. [11]

12. *Concerning Sin, and the Attitude to Take if We Find We are in Sin*

In fact, to have sinned is no sin if one regrets it. A man should not wish to commit a sin for all that can happen in time or eternity — neither mortal nor venial nor any kind of sin. He who is wise in the ways of God should ever consider that our faithful and loving God has brought us from a sinful life to a godly life: out of an enemy He has made a friend, which is more than to have created a new earth. This should be one of the main reasons why a man should establish himself firmly in God, and it would amaze you how greatly this would inspire a man in strong deep love, so that he would renounce himself completely.

Indeed, a man truly established in God's will should not wish that the sin into which he had fallen had never been: not in the sense that it was against God, but because thereby you are bound to greater love and thus made lowly and humble — even though it was against God. But you should safely trust God not to have permitted this unless He wanted to turn it to your profit. But when a man stands right above sin and turns completely away, then our faithful God acts as if that man had never fallen into sin, and will not let him suffer for a moment for all his sins. Even if they were as many as all men have ever committed, God will never punish him, but would be as familiar to that man as to any other creature. Provided He finds him now ready, He pays no regard to what he was before. God is a God of the present. As He finds you, so He takes and receives you, not as what you were but as what you are now. All the harm and shame that God can bear on account of all sins, He will gladly bear and have borne for many a year, so that a man may come to a greater recognition of His love, and so that that man's love and gratitude may be the greater, and his zeal the hotter, as indeed is the right and frequent outcome after one has sinned.

That is why God gladly accepts the harm of sins and has often tolerated it and allowed it to come to those whom He has chosen to prepare for great things. See: who was dearer to our Lord or more intimate with him than the Apostles were? Yet not one of them but fell into mortal sin: they had all been mortal sinners. He has frequently shown this in both the Old and the New Testament in regard to those who afterwards were by far the dearest to Him; and even now one seldom finds that people come to greatness without erring somewhat at first. Our Lord's intention in this is that we should recognise his great mercy: he wants to urge us by this to great and true humility and devotion. For when repentance is renewed, love too is greatly increased and renewed.

13. *Of Two Kinds of Repentance*

There are two kinds of repentance. The one is temporal or sensible, the other is divine and supernatural. Temporal repentance drags down into ever greater sorrow and plunges a man into such distress that he is ready to despair, and then the repentance remains painful and gets no further: nothing comes of this.

But divine repentance is quite different. As soon as a man feels dissatisfied, he at once rises towards God and establishes an unshakeable will to turn from all sin for ever; then he lifts himself in full confidence to God and gains great assurance;

and from that there arises a spiritual joy which elevates the soul above all woe and distress and makes it fast to God. For the more a man feels himself at fault and the more he has sinned, the greater reason he has to bind himself with undivided love to God, with whom there is no sin and no lack. And so, the best step a man can take if he would come to God in full devotion, is to be without sin in divine repentance.

And the greater we ourselves feel our sin to be, the more ready God is to forgive that sin and to enter the soul to drive it out; for everyone is most eager to get rid of what hurts him most. So, the more and the greater the sins, the more immeasurably glad and the quicker God is to forgive them, the more so since they are more hateful to Him. [12] And then, when this divine repentance lifts itself up to God, all sins have vanished in God's abyss more quickly than I can blink an eye, and they are completely destroyed as if they had never been, provided the repentance is complete.

14. *Of True Confidence and Hope*

The sign of perfect love is if one has great hope and trust in God; for there is no better sign of perfect love than trust. For if a man deeply and perfectly loves another, that creates trust, and whatever one dares to expect of God one will really find, and a thousandfold more. And so, just as God could never love a man too much, nor could a man trust God too much. Of all things a man can do, none is so seemly as putting full trust in God. There was none who ever had full confidence in Him but He wrought great things with them. And He has proved to all men that this confidence comes from love, for love has not only confidence, it has true knowledge and indubitable security.

31

15. *Of Two Kinds of Certainty of Eternal Life*

There are in this life two kinds of certainty of eternal life. One is when God tells a man Himself or through an angel or shows him by a special illumination. This happens seldom and to few. [13] The other kind of knowledge is incomparably better, and this often comes to people who have perfect love. It is when a man's love and intimacy with God are such that he has such perfect trust and security in Him, that he cannot doubt and is thus quite assured, loving Him without distinction in all creatures. And even if all creatures rejected him and forswore him, though God Himself rejected him, he would not lose his faith, for love *cannot* lose faith but always trusts in the good. Nor is there any need to say a word to the lover or the beloved, for by knowing him to be His friend God at once knows all that is good for him and pertains to his felicity. For however much you love Him, rest assured that He loves you immeasurably more and has vastly more faith in you. For He is good faith in Himself; of this you and all who love Him may be assured.

This assurance is far greater, more perfect and truer than the first, and cannot deceive us. But the telling [i.e. the first kind mentioned above] might be deceptive and could be a false illumination. But *this* one is felt in all the powers of the soul and cannot deceive those who truly love God; they doubt as little as that man doubts God, for love drives out fear. [14]

"Love knows not fear", as St John says (1 John 4:18; [15] and it is also written: "Love covers a multitude of sins" (1 Peter 4:8). For when sins occur there can be no perfect trust or love because this covers up sin, it knows nothing of sin. Not that one has not sinned, but that it totally destroys and banishes sin as if it had never been. For all God's works are absolutely perfect and superabundant, so that if He forgives He forgives altogether and completely, and more willingly big sins than little, and that creates perfect faith. I consider this far better, incomparably better than the former knowing, and it brings a greater reward and is truer, for nothing hinders it, neither sin nor anything else. For when God finds men in equal love, He judges them equally, even though one may have sinned much or not at all. But he to whom more is forgiven should love the more, as our Lord Christ said: "He to whom more is forgiven must love more" (Luke 7:47).

16. *Of True Penance and Holy Living*
Many people think they are performing great works by outward things such as fasting, going barefoot, or other such things which are called penance. But the true and best penance is that whereby one improves greatly and in the highest degree; and that is that a man should experience a complete and perfect turning away from whatever is not entirely God and divine in himself and in all creatures, and have a full, perfect and complete turning towards his beloved God in unshakeable love, so that his devotion and yearning for Him are great. In whatever you do, the more of this is present, the more righteous you are; and the more this is the case, in the same measure will there be more penance, and it will wash away more sin and all pain. Indeed, you might well turn away quickly and in a short time from all sins, so strongly and with such true revulsion, and turn so strongly to God that, though you had committed all the sins that ever were or shall be since Adam's time, they would all be forgiven you, together with the punishment for them, so that if you were to die now you would come before the face of God. This

is true penance, and it comes especially and most perfectly through true suffering in the perfect penance of our Lord Jesus Christ. The more a man enters into that, the more all sin, and all penalties of sin, drop away from him. And a man should so train himself in all his actions as always to grow into the life and works of our Lord Jesus Christ, in all his doing and leaving undone, enduring and living, being ever mindful of him here as he was mindful of us.

This penance is truly a state of mind lifted into God away from all things, and in whatever works you find you can have it most, and have it from those works, do them the more freely; and then, if any outward work should hinder you, whether it be fasting, watching, reading or whatever else, you can safely leave that alone without worrying about failing in any penance. For God regards not what the works are, but only what love and devotion and what kind of a spirit is in the works. For He is little concerned with our works, but only with our state of mind in all our works, that we love Him alone in all things. For a man is too greedy if he is not satisfied with God. All your works shall be rewarded in that God knows of them and that you intend Him in them; let that ever suffice you. And the more purely and simply you seek God in them, the more truly will your works atone for your sins.

You should consider, too, that God was the common saviour of the entire world, and for that I owe Him more gratitude than if He had saved me alone. Thus you should be a common saviour of all that you have spoilt in yourself by sin; and you must commit yourself to Him with all that, for with sin you have spoilt all that is in you — heart, mind, body, soul, powers and whatever else there is in and about you: it is all sick and spoilt. Therefore flee to Him, in whom is no fault, but all is good, that He may be to you a common saviour of all your rottenness within and without.

17. *How a Man Should Rest in Peace When not Oppressed by Outward Distress Such as Christ and the Saints Often Endured; and How He Should Follow God*

People may well be daunted and afraid because the life of our Lord Jesus Christ and the saints was so severe and painful, and a man cannot endure much of this or does not feel compelled to it. And so, when people feel themselves unequal to this, they often think they are far from God, as One whom they are unable to follow. No one should think this. A man should in no wise ever deem himself far from God, whether on account of failings or of weakness or for anything. Even suppose, though, that your great shortcomings have carried you so far away that you cannot conceive yourself near to God, you should still regard God as near to you. For great harm results if a man puts God at a distance: for whether a man goes near or far, God never goes far away but always stands nearby; and even if He cannot remain within, He never goes further than outside the door.

It is the same with the strictness of your imitation. [16] Now see how your imitation should be. You should note and have paid attention to what God has chiefly enjoined you to do, for not all people are called to God by the same route, as St Paul says (cf. 1 Cor. 7:24). If you then find that your nearest way is not in the doing of outward works or in great endurance or deprivation — which are actually of small account unless a man is specially driven to them by God or has the power to perform them without damage to his inner life — if you find that this is not in you, then be at peace and do not take much of this upon yourself.

But you may say: 'If this does not matter, then why did our forbears, many of them saints, do it?' Consider this: our Lord gave them this way and also the strength to do it, so that they *could* follow this way, and he was pleased with them for this, in which they should profit best. For God has not bound man's salvation to any special mode. Whatever has one mode has not another, but God has endowed all good ways with effectiveness and denied this to no good way.[17] For one good does not conflict with another good. And so people should observe that they do wrong if they see or hear of a good man, and because he does not follow their way they consider it is all wasted. If they don't like people's ways they disregard their *good* way and good intent, which is not right. We should have more regard to other people's way, when they have true devotion, and not scorn anybody's way.

Let every man keep to his own good way and include all ways in it, and take up in his way *all* goodness and all ways. To change one's way makes for instability of mind as well as of way. Whatever you can get from one way you can also obtain from another if it is good and praiseworthy and mindful only of God: but not all men can follow one path. And so it is with imitating the austerities of such saints. You should love this way, and it may well appeal to you, even though you need not follow it.

Now you might say: 'Our Lord Jesus Christ always had the highest way, we ought to follow *him*.' That is true. We certainly should follow our Lord, but not in all respects. Our Lord fasted for forty days, but no one should take it upon himself to follow that. Christ performed many works in which he intended that we should follow him spiritually but not physically. And so one should endeavour to follow him sensibly, for he sought our love more than our deeds. We must follow him in our own way. 'Such as?' — Pay attention in all things how, and in what way. [18] As I have often said, I consider a spiritual work more valuable than a physical one.

'How is that?' — Christ fasted for forty days. Follow him this way, by observing whatever you are most inclined to or ready for: concentrate on that and observe yourself closely. Often it is more necessary for you freely to renounce *that*, than if you were to give up all food. And sometimes it is harder for you to keep silence about a single word than to cease speaking altogether. And sometimes, too, it is harder for a man to endure a single word of reproach, which means nothing, than a fierce blow that he was prepared for; or it is much harder for him to be alone in a crowd than in the desert; or he finds it harder to abandon a small thing than a great, or to do a small task than one which is considered much greater. In this way a man can well follow our Lord (even) in his weakness, without feeling or needing to feel himself far removed.

18. *In What Way a Man May Take as is Fitting, Delicate Food and Fine Clothing and Merry Companions if They Attach Themselves to Him in the Natural Course*

You need not worry about food and drink, as to whether they seem too good for you, but train your ground and your mind to be far above such things. Let nothing touch your mind with power and love but God alone — it should be exalted above all else. Why? Because that would be a feeble kind of inwardness that the outward dress could correct. Rather should the inward correct the outer, if it rests entirely with you. But if it just comes to you, you can from your ground accept it as good, just as you would put up with it if it were different, and would be glad and willing to endure it. The same applies to food, friends and relations and with whatever else God gives you or takes from you.

And that I consider better than anything, that a man should fully abandon himself to God when He would cast anything upon him, be it disgrace, trouble or whatever kind of suffering it might be, accepting it with joy and gratitude, allowing oneself rather to be led by God than plunging into it oneself. So just learn all things gladly from God and follow Him, and all will go well with you. In that way you can well take honour or comfort, but in such a way that, if discomfort and dishonour were to be a man's lot, he would likewise be able and willing to bear them. *Then* they may rightly and legitimately feast, who would have been as ready and willing to fast.[19] And that is doubtless why God spares His friends much great suffering; for otherwise His measureless good faith would not permit this, seeing that so much great profit resides in suffering, and He would not and ought not to deprive them of any good thing. He is satisfied with the good will, otherwise He would not omit any suffering, on account of the innumerable benefits suffering brings.

And so, so long as God is satisfied, rest content: and when something different pleases Him in regard to you, be also content. For a man should inwardly be so wholly for God with all his will, that he should worry little about the way or about works. In particular you should eschew all, whether in clothing, food or speech — such as using high-flown words — or any peculiarity of gestures, which is of no value. Still, you must know that not *all* peculiarity is forbidden. There are forms of singularity that must be maintained at times and with many people, for he who is singular must also behave unusually many times and in many ways.

A man should have conformed himself to our Lord Jesus Christ inwardly in all things, so that in him is found a reflection of all his works and of his divine image; so a man should bear within himself a perfect likeness, as far as he can, of all his works. You must work and he must take. Do your work with perfect devotion and with full intent; train your mind to this at all times so as to conform in all things to him.

19. *Why God Often Allows Good People, Who are Truly Good, to be Prevented from Doing Good Works*

God in His faithfulness often permits His friends to succumb to weakness to the end that whatever support they might lean on or cling to may give way. For to a loving soul it would be great joy if he could perform many and great feats, whether in keeping vigil, in fasting or in other practices, or in some especial great and difficult undertakings. This is a great joy, support and hope for them, so that their works become their mainstay, support and security. Our Lord does not want this, for *he* wishes to be their sole support and security. And he does this solely out of his goodness and compassion. For nothing moves God to any act but His own goodness, and our deeds contribute nothing to making God give us anything or do anything for us. Our Lord wants his friends to abandon this attitude, so he deprives them of this support in order that he alone may be their support. For he wants to endow them richly for no other reason than from his free goodness, and he would be their support and consolation. But they should consider and regard themselves as mere nothing in all God's great gifts; for the more barely and freely the mind falls on to God and is supported by Him, the more deeply a man is established in God and the more receptive to God in all His most precious gifts. For a man should build on God alone.

20. *Of the Body of Our Lord, That One Should Receive It Often, and in What Way and Frame of Mind*

Whoever would fain receive the body of our Lord has no need to attend to what he experiences or tastes in it, or how great his piety and reverence is, but he should observe how his will and intention is. You should not overestimate your feelings, but rather have due respect for that which you love and strive for.

A man who is freely able and willing to go to our Lord should first of all be in such a state that his conscience is free from all reproach of sin. The second thing is that a man's will should be turned to God, so that he seeks nothing and desires nothing but God and all that is divine, and that he is displeased with what is unlike God. For that is the test of how far or how near a man is to God: according as he has more or less of this. The third thing he should have is that his love for the sacrament and our Lord should grow more and more, and that his reverent awe should not diminish by frequent going. For often, what is one man's life is another man's death. And so you should note in yourself whether your love for God grows and your reverence is not extinguished. *Then*, the more often you go to the sacrament the better you will be, and it will also be of greater benefit and profit to you. Therefore, do not let anyone put you off God by talk or preaching, for the more the better and the more pleasing to God. For our Lord revels in dwelling in and with man.

But you might say: 'Alas, sir, I feel so bare and cold and lazy that I dare not face our Lord!' I reply: All the more need for you to go to your God, for by Him you will be enflamed and set afire, and in Him you will be sanctified and joined and made one with Him, for you will find such grace in the sacrament, and nowhere else so truly, that your bodily powers are there united and collected by the precious power of the physical presence of our Lord's body, so that all a man's scattered senses and his mind are here concentrated and unified, and those which especially were too much inclined downward will be lifted up and duly offered to God. And by the indwelling God they will be so inwardly trained and weaned of the bodily hindrances of temporal things and limbered up towards divine things, and so, strengthened by God's body, *your* body will be renewed. For we should be turned into Him and become fully united with Him, so that His own becomes ours, and ours all becomes His: our heart and His one heart and our body and His one body. Thus our senses and our will, intention, our powers and our limbs are borne into Him so that we sense and become aware of Him in all the powers of body and soul.

But you might say: 'Alas, sir, I know of no great matters in me, only poverty. How dare I go to Him like this?' Truly, if you want to transform all your poverty, then go to the abundant treasury of immeasurable riches, and you will be rich. For you must know that He alone is the treasure which can sate you and fill you full. Therefore say: 'I will go to You, that Your riches may end my penury and all Your boundless superfluity fill up my emptiness, and Your immeasurable, inconceivable Godhead replenish my all too base and corrupt humanity.'

41

'Alas, sir, I have sinned greatly, I cannot atone.' Therefore go to him, for he has nobly atoned for all sins. In him you may offer the precious sacrifice to the heavenly Father for all your guilt.

'Alas, sir, I would gladly praise him, but I cannot.' Go to him, for he alone is the thank-offering acceptable to the Father and a measureless, truthful and perfect praise of all God's goodness.

In short, if you would be at once rid of all defects and be clothed in virtue and grace, or be joyously led and conducted to the source, then conduct yourself in such a way that you can take the sacrament worthily and often, and then you will be united with him and ennobled with his body. Indeed, in the body of our Lord the soul is so joined to God that all angels, whether of the choir of Cherubim or of Seraphim, cannot discover or find out the difference between them. For wherever they touch God they touch the soul, and where they touch the soul they touch God. There never was so close a union, for the soul is far more closely united with God than are body and soul, which make up a man. This union is far closer than when a man pours a drop of water into a vat of wine, for that would make water and wine — but *this* is so turned into one that all creatures could never find out the difference.[20]

But you might say, 'How can that be? I can't feel anything.' What matter? The less you feel and the more you firmly believe, the more laudable is your faith, and the more it will be respected and praised, for perfect faith is far more in a man than mere belief. In it we have true knowing. In fact we lack nothing but true faith. If we think we get more from one thing than from another, that is due to outward conventions, for one thing is not greater than another. Thus he who has equal faith takes equally and has things equally. [21]

But you might say, 'How can I believe in higher things as long as I do not feel in such a condition, but feel myself imperfect and prone to many things?' Just see. You should observe two things in yourself which our Lord also had in himself. He possessed the higher and the lower powers, which had two different functions. His higher powers had possession and enjoyment of eternal bliss. But His lower powers were at the same time involved in the greatest suffering and struggle in the world, yet none of these works hindered the others in their sphere. [22] That is how it should be in you, that the highest powers should be lifted entirely into God, and entirely surrendered and added to Him. Moreover, we should assign all suffering to the body, to the lower powers and the senses, but the spirit should raise itself up with all its strength and plunge unfettered into God. Rather, the suffering of the senses and the lower powers are not your concern, nor this assault of the world: for the greater and fiercer the struggle, the greater and more glorious the victory and the honour of victory. For the greater the temptation and stronger the assault of vice, if a man yet prevails, the more truly is the virtue yours and the dearer to your God. Therefore, if you would be worthy to receive God, look to it that your highest powers are directed to God and that your will ever seeks His, and consider what you want from Him and how your loyalty is towards Him. [23]

No man ever receives the precious body of our Lord in this spirit without receiving great and especial grace, and the oftener, the greater the profit. Indeed, it is possible for a man to receive the body of our Lord with such devotion and intentness that if he were ordained to enter the lowest choir of angels, by once receiving him thus he would be raised to the next choir; in fact you could receive him with such devotion that you would be deemed worthy to enter the eighth or ninth choir.[24] And so, if there were two men, alike in their lives, and if one of them had worthily received the body of our Lord once more than the other, that man would thereby be as a bright sun above the other and have a special union with God.

This receiving and this blessed enjoyment of the body of our Lord depends not just on outward enjoyment, it depends too on spiritual enjoyment with desirous mind, in at-onement and devotion. It is possible for a man to receive this so faithfully that he is richer in blessings than anyone on earth. A man can do this a thousand times a day or more, wherever he is, whether he is ill or well. However, it is necessary to fit oneself for this in sacramental fashion, according to wise and proper order and in accordance with the magnitude of one's desire for it. But if one has not the desire one should urge oneself on, make ready and conduct oneself accordingly, and then one can become holy in time and blessed in eternity: for to follow and obey God *is* eternity. May the Teacher of truth grant us this, and the love of chastity and the life of eternal bliss. Amen.

21. *Of Diligence*

Whenever a man wishes to receive the body of our Lord, he may well approach without undue worry. But it is seemly and very profitable to confess first, even if one has no pangs of conscience, for the sake of the fruits of the sacrament of confession. But should a man have some compunction, and if on account of preoccupation he cannot go to confession, let him go to his God, confess himself guilty with true repentance, and be at peace until he has a chance to go to confession. And if during this the thought or pangs of conscience for his sins disappear, he may consider that God has also forgotten them. One should rather confess to God than to man, and it is a duty to take one's confession to God seriously and accuse oneself strictly. Nor should a man who intends to go to the sacrament lightly abandon this and leave it aside for the sake of some outward penance, for it is a man's intention in his works that is righteous, godly and good.

You should learn to be unattached in your works. But for an unpractised man it is an uncommon thing to reach the point where no crowd and no task hinders him — it calls for diligent application — so that God is ever present to him and shines before him completely unveiled, at all times and in all company.[25] Skilful diligence is required for this, and in particular two things. One is that a man has shut himself off well inwardly, so that his mind is on its guard against the images without, that they remain without and do not unfittingly keep company and walk with him, and that they find no resting-place in him. The second is that he should not let himself be caught up by his *internal* imagery, whether it be in the form of pictures or lofty thoughts, or outward impressions or whatever is present to his mind, nor be distracted nor dissipate himself in their multiplicity. A man should train and bend all his powers to this and keep his inner self present to him.

Now you might say a man must turn outwards if he is to do external works, for no task can be done but according to its own form.[26] That is true. But the externality of form is nothing external for the practised man, for to the inward-turned man all things have an inward divinity. This above all is necessary: that a man should train and practise his mind well and bring it to God, and then he will always have divinity within. Nothing is so proper to the intellect, nor so present and near as God. It never turns in any other direction. It does not turn to creatures unless subjected to violence and injustice, whereby it is quite broken and perverted. If it is thus spoilt in a young person, or whoever it may be, it must be very diligently trained, and it is necessary to do all in one's power to bring the intellect back and train it. For, however proper and natural God is to it, once it gets turned away and is settled among creatures and caught up in them and accustomed to this state, it becomes so weakened in this part and lacking in self-control, so hindered in its noble striving, that all a man's efforts are insufficient to draw it back fully. Even though he makes every effort, he requires constant watchfulness.

Above all things a man must see to it that he trains himself strictly and well. If an untrained, unpractised man wanted to conduct himself and behave like a trained man, he would destroy himself and nothing would ever come of him. Once a man has first quite weaned himself of all things and become a stranger to them, *then* he can faithfully perform all his tasks, and delight in them or leave them alone without hindrance. But whatever a man loves or takes pleasure in and wilfully follows, whether it be food or drink or anything else, this cannot be maintained without harm in an untrained man. A man must train himself not to seek his own in anything, but to find and take God in all things. For God does not give, and has never given any gift which a man might take and rest content with it. All the gifts He has ever given in heaven and on earth, He gave that He might give one gift — Himself. With all these gifts He wishes to prepare us for that gift which is Himself; and all the works God ever wrought in heaven or on earth He wrought for the sake of working one work — to hallow Himself that He might hallow us. Therefore I say, in all gifts and in all works we must learn to regard God; we should be satisfied with nothing and stop nowhere. There is no manner of standing still for us in this life, and never has been for any man, however advanced he might be. Above all things, a man must ever be directed towards God's gifts, and ever anew.

I will speak briefly of one who greatly wished to receive something from our Lord. I said she was not yet ready, and if God gave her the gift while she was unready, it would perish. A question: 'Why was she not ready? She had a good will, and you say that that can do all things, and it contains all things and all perfection.' That is true; but there are two different meanings of 'will': the one is an accidental and non-essential will, and the other is a decisive will, a creative and a trained will. Of course it is not sufficient for a man's mind to be detached for one split second, just when he wants to link up with God, but one must have a well-trained detachment before and after. *Then* one can receive great things from God, and God in those things. But if one is not ready, the gift is spoilt, and God with the gift. That is why God cannot always give us things as we ask for them. It is not due to a lack on His part, for He is a thousand times more eager to give to us than we are to receive. But we do Him violence and wrong in hindering His natural work by our unreadiness.

A man must learn to give up self in all gifts, and keep or seek nothing for himself, not profit or enjoyment or inwardness or sweetness or reward or heaven or own-will. God never gave Himself and never will give Himself in another's will: He only gives Himself in His own will. Where God finds His own will, there He gives Himself and bestows Himself in it with all that He is. And the more we die to our own, the more truly we come to be in *that*.[27] Therefore it is not enough for Him that we give up self and all we have and can do just once, but we must constantly renew ourselves and so make ourselves simple and free in all things.

It is also very useful for a man not to be satisfied to possess virtues in his mind such as obedience, poverty, and the rest; but he should practise the works and fruits of virtue, often putting himself to the test, and be willing and anxious to be trained and tested by people. For it is not enough to perform works of virtue, or practise obedience or endure poverty and disgrace, or humble and abandon ourselves in some other way — we must strive and never cease until we have gained the virtue in its essence and ground. And the test of the matter is this: if we feel inclined to virtue above all else, and perform virtuous deeds without preparation of the will, and carry them through without the special spur of a just or important cause, when in fact virtue performs itself more by itself and for love of virtue without any why or wherefore — *then* one has the perfection of virtue, and not before.

We must school ourselves in abandoning till we keep nothing back. All turbulence and unrest comes from self-will, whether we know it or not. We should place ourselves with all we have in a pure renunciation[28] of will and desire, into the good and precious will of God, together with everything that we may will or desire in any form.

A question: 'Should one willingly forgo all God's sweetness? May this not easily stem from laziness or insufficient love of God?' Certainly, if one does not understand the difference. For we can tell whether it comes from laziness or from true detachment and self-abandonment by observing whether, when we feel in this state, when we feel inwardly completely detached, we are just as much devoted to God as if we felt Him most strongly; if we do in this state just what we should do — no more and no less — keeping free and detached from all comfort and help, as we should do when we were aware of God's presence.

For a man in a right state in perfect good will, no time can be too short. For if the will is such that it wills totally all that it can — not only now but, even if a man endured a thousand years he would will to do all in his power — that will performs as much as could be achieved in works in a thousand years: he has done it all in the sight of God.

22. How We Ought to Follow God, and About Good Ways

A man who would start on a new life or work should betake himself to his God, and beg Him with all his might and with total devotion to dispose things for the best, as shall best please and honour God, seeking in it nothing of his own but merely God's dearest will and nothing else. Whatever God then sends him, let him take it direct from God, regard it as best for himself, and be fully content.

Though later on some other way may please him better, he should think: 'This is the way God has sent you', and accept it as the best. He should trust God in this and bring all good ways into line with this, taking all things in and according to this, whatever their nature. For whatever good God has done and given in one way, can be found in all good ways. For in one way one should take all good ways and not cling to the peculiarities of the way. For a man must always do one thing, he cannot do everything. It must always be one thing, and in that *one* one should take everything. For if a man wanted to do everything, this and that, dropping his way for another's way, which he liked better, truly that would make for great instability. For that man would reach perfection sooner who left the world to join one order only, than he ever would who should leave one order for another, however holy. That comes of changing ways. Let a man choose a good way and keep to it, introducing all good ways into it and bearing in mind that it comes from God, instead of starting one thing today and something else tomorrow; he need not worry that he is missing anything. For with God one can miss nothing. With God one can no more miss anything than God can miss anything. So, take one way from God, and embody in it all good things.

But if it turns out that they are incompatible, one at variance with the other, then you have a sure sign that it is not from God. One good is not foe to another, for, as our Lord said: "A kingdom divided against itself will not stand" (Luke 11:17). He also said: "Whoever is not with me is against me, and he who does not gather up with me, scatters" (Luke 11:23). So let this be a sure sign: whatever good does not tolerate, or destroys, another good, even a lesser good, is not from God. It should bring increase, not destroy.

In a few brief and true words, then, there is no doubt that God in His faithfulness takes every man at his best. That is assuredly so, and He never takes a man lying down whom He might have found standing up, for God intends the best for all things. I was asked why, in that case, God does not take those who — He knows — will fall away from the grace of baptism, so that they might die in childhood, before reaching discretion, since He is aware that they will fall and not rise again — for would not that be best for them? I reply that God is not a destroyer of any good, but a fulfiller: God is not nature's destroyer, but her fulfiller. Even grace does not destroy nature but fulfils it. [29] Now if God destroyed Nature in the beginning, he would do her harm and outrage, and that He does not do. Man has freewill to choose good or evil, and God lays before him death for evil and life for doing good. Man should be free, lord of all his deeds, undestroyed and uncompelled. Grace does not destroy nature, but fulfils it, for glory is fulfilled grace. [30] Thus there is nothing in God that destroys anything that has being, but he is a fulfiller of all things. Therefore we should not destroy any small good in ourselves, nor a small way by a greater, but we should fulfil it in the highest.

I have been speaking about one who wanted to begin a new life right from the beginning, and I said this: that a man should become a God-seeker in all things and a God-finder at all times, in all places, in all company, in all ways. In this manner one can always incessantly wax and grow, and never reach an end of growth.

23. *Of Inward and Outward Works*
Suppose a man should withdraw into himself with all his powers, outward and inward, then when he is in that condition there is in him no image or motive, and he is without any activity within or without. Then he should well

51

observe whether there is any inclination towards anything. But if a man is not drawn to any work and does not want to undertake anything, then he should force himself into some activity, whether inward or outward (for a man should not be satisfied with anything, however good it may seem or be) so that, when he finds himself oppressed or constrained, it may appear rather that that man *is worked* than that he *works*; thus he may learn to co-operate with his God. Not that one should give up or neglect or reject one's inner life, but in it and with it and from it one should learn to act in such a way as to let the inward break into activity and draw the activity into inwardness, and thereby train oneself to act in freedom. For one should turn one's eyes to this inner work and act therefrom, whether it be in reading, praying or — on occasion — outward work. But if the outward work tends to destroy the inward, one should follow the inward. But if both can be as one, that is best, then one is co-operating with God. You ask: 'How can there be co-operation, if a man has become lost to self and all activities and, as St Dionysius[31] says, he speaks most fairly of God who in the fullness of interior riches can best hold his peace — then image and work, praise and thanks or whatever he may do disappear?' One answer: one work yet truly and genuinely belongs to him, and that is the destruction of self. But this naughting and shrinking of self is never so great but it lacks something unless God Himself completes it in us. Only then is humility sufficient, when God humbles a man with that man, and only then is that man, and the virtue, perfected, and not before.

A question: 'How does God destroy a man with himself? It would seem that the destruction of man would be his exaltation by God, for the gospel says: "He that humbles

himself shall be exalted" (Matt. 23:12, Luke 14:11).'
Answer: Yes and no. He must humble himself, and this
cannot be done sufficiently unless God does it: and he shall be
exalted, not that the humbling is one thing and the exalting
another, but the highest height of exaltation lies in the deep
ground of humility. For the deeper and lower the ground, the
higher and more immeasurable the exaltation and the height.
The deeper the well, the higher it is; height and depth are
one. And so, whoever can humble himself more is raised
higher, and therefore our Lord said: "He who desires to be the
greatest, let him be the least among you" (Mark 9:34). He
who would become this must become that. *This* being is
found only in *that* becoming. He who becomes least *is* truly
the greatest; but he who has *become* least is truly now the very
greatest. Thus the word of the evangelist is made true and
fulfilled: "He that humbles himself shall be exalted." For our
whole being depends on nothing but a becoming-nothing.

It is written: "They have become rich in all virtues" (cf.
1 Cor. 1:5). Truly, this can never happen unless we first
become poor in all things. He who would receive all things
must abandon all things. This is fair dealing and an equal
bargain, as I said long ago. Therefore, when God wishes to
give us Himself and all things in free possession, He wishes to
take from us, once and for all, all possessiveness. Truly, God
would not in any way that we should possess as much as
might fill my eyes. For of all the gifts He ever gave us, gifts of
nature or of grace, He never gave any but so that we might
possess nothing of our own, for such possession he has not
granted in any way, to His Mother, to any man or any
creature. And in order to teach us this or to make us ready for
this, He frequently takes from us both physical and spiritual

goods, for the possession of honour should not be ours, but only His. Rather we should hold all things as if they were lent to us and not given, without possessiveness, whether it be body or soul, senses, powers, outward goods or honours, friends, relations, hearth and home, or anything at all.

What is God's purpose that He insists so much on this? He wishes Himself to be our sole and perfect possession. This He wills and intends, and this alone he strives for, that He can and may be this. In this lies His greatest joy and delight. And the more, and the more fully this is so, the greater His joy and happiness; for the more we possess of things the less we possess of Him, and the less love we have of things, the more we have of Him with all that He can do. Therefore, when our Lord wanted to speak of all blessings, he put poverty of spirit as the crown of them all, and this was their chief (Matt. 5:3) as a sign that all bliss and perfection always start with poverty of spirit, and that was in truth a foundation on which to build all that is good, which could not exist without it.

In return for our keeping ourselves free of all things external to ourselves, God will give us free possession of all that is in heaven, and heaven itself with all its power; indeed, whatever flowed from Him that all the angels and saints have, to be ours as it is theirs, far more than any *thing* is mine. In return for my going out of myself for His sake, God will be mine entirely with all that He is and can do, as much mine as His, no more and no less. He will be a thousand times more my own than whatever any man ever had and kept in a chest, or than he ever belonged to himself. Nothing was ever so much my own as God will be mine with all that He is and can do.

We must earn this possession here by not possessing

ourselves or anything that is not God, and the more perfect and free this poverty, the greater the possession. But we should never aim at, or think of this return, our eyes should never once look to see if we are ever to gain or receive anything, but solely for the love of virtue. For the more detached, the more truly possessed, as the noble St Paul says we ought to have "as having nothing, yet possessing all things" (2 Cor. 6:10). He is without possession, who does not desire or wish to have anything of himself or of all that is outside of him, or even of God or anything.

Do you want to know who is a truly poor man? That man is truly poor in spirit who can do without anything unnecessary. That is why he who sat naked in his tub[32] said to Alexander the Great, to whom the whole world was subject: 'I am a greater ruler than you, for I have rejected more things than you have ever possessed. What you think it a great thing to possess, is too petty for me to scorn.' He is far more blessed who can do without all things and have no need of them, than he who has possession of all things and has wants. That man is the best who can do without what he does not need. Therefore he who can do without and despise the most has abandoned most. It seems a great thing if a man gives up a thousand marks of gold for God's sake and builds many hermitages and monasteries and feeds all the poor: that would be a great deed. But he would be far more blessed who should despise as much for God's sake. That man would possess very heaven who could for God's sake renounce all things, whatever God gave or did not give.

You may say, 'Yes, sir, but would I not be a cause of hindrance through my failings?' If you have failings, then pray frequently to God, if it is to His Glory and if it suits

Him, to free you from them, for without Him you can do nothing. If He takes them away, thank Him: if He does not, then you suffer for His sake, not as the weakness of sin, but rather as a great training whereby you can earn a reward, and practise patience. You should be satisfied, whether He gives you His gift or not.

God gives every man according to what is best and most fitting for him. If you want to make a coat for a man you have to make it to his measure; what fits one would not fit another at all. So we measure each one to see what fits him. Thus God gives to every man the best according as He perceives what is most necessary for him. Indeed, anyone who has full trust in God in this regard receives and gets as much from the smallest gift as from the greatest. If God wanted to give me what He gave St Paul,[33] I would accept it gladly, if He wished it. But since He will not give it to me — for He wants very few people to know in this world what St Paul knew — then the fact that God does not give it to me is just as dear to me, and I thank Him as much and am as satisfied that He witholds it as I would be if He had granted it; and I am as content and happy as if He had done so, if in other respects I am in a right state. In truth, I should be satisfied with God's will: whatever God wished to do or give, I should be so pleased and should prize that will no less than if He gave me the gift and performed the deed in me. Then all gifts would be mine, and all God's works, and whether all creatures were to do their best or their worst, they could not deprive me of that. Why should I complain, when the gifts of all men are mine? Truly I would be so satisfied with whatever God did to me, or whatever He gave me or did not give me, that I would not give a brass farthing to gain the kind of life I might imagine to be the best.

You may say, 'I fear I am not earnest enough and don't try as hard as I could.' You should regret this and endure it with patience; regard it as discipline and be at peace. God gladly endures shame and misfortune and willingly forgoes His praise and service that those who love Him and belong to Him may be at peace. Why should we then not be at peace, whatever He gives us or whatever we lack? Thus it is written, and our Lord says: "Blessed are they who suffer for righteousness' sake" (Matt. 5:10). Indeed, if a thief about to be hanged, who had well deserved it by his thefts, or one who had committed murder and was justly to be executed, could find it in themselves to say, 'Look, you are going to suffer this for righteousness' sake, it serves you right', they would be saved immediately. In fact, however wrong we may be, if we duly accept from God whatever He does or does not do to us, and suffer for righteousness' sake, we are blessed. Therefore do not lament for anything, but bewail only the fact that you still do lament and are not satisfied. You should only lament that you have too much. For he who was in a right state would take it all the same way, lacking and having.

Now you will say, 'Well, God performs such great things in many people, and thus they are overshadowed by the divine being, and God works in them, not they themselves.' Thank God for their sake, and if He grants it to you, in God's name take it; if He does not, then willingly do without, and seek nothing but Him, and be unconcerned as to whether God does your deeds or you do; for God *must* do them if you seek only Him — whether He wants to or not.

Do not bother yourself about what condition or way of life God gives anyone. If I were so good and holy that I were to be elevated among the saints, people would talk about it, and speculate whether it was a matter of nature or of grace, and get confused. They were wrong to do that. Let God work in you, give Him the work and do not worry about whether He works with nature or above nature: both nature and grace are His. What does it matter to you how it suits Him to work, or what work He performs in you or in someone else? He must work how, where and in whatever way it suits Him.

A man very much wanted to conduct a stream into his garden and said: 'As long as I get the water, I don't care what kind of pipe it comes through, whether it is of iron or wood, of bone or rusty metal, provided the water comes through.' And so they are all wrong who worry about *how* God works in you, whether by nature or by grace. Just leave the work to Him, and you be at peace.

For as far as you are in God, you are at peace, and as far as you are out of God, you are not at peace. If anything is in God, it has peace: as much in God, so much at peace. That is how you can tell how far you are in God or otherwise, by whether you have peace or unrest. For where you have unrest, you *must* be restless, for unrest comes from creatures and not from God. Nor is there anything to be feared in God: whatever is in God is to be loved. Likewise, there is nothing in Him to cause sadness.

Whoever has all his will and what he wants is joyful. No one has that but he whose will and God's will are one. God grant us this oneness. Amen.

Notes

1. Cf. No. 13b (I, p. 118).
2. *Conf.* X, ch. 26 (Q).

3. Reading *menige* 'crowd' with Q (rejecting Pfeiffer's conjecture *meinunge* 'opinion').

4. Cf. No. 57 (II, p. 87).

5. St Gregory the Great, *Homilies* (PL 76, 1093) (Q).

6. Cf. No. 15 (I, p. 103f.).

7. On the difficulty of translating Eckhart's *glîch*, see No. 65 (II, pp. 131ff. and n. 10).

8. Not in the sense of the 'Friends of God' (*Gottesfreunde*) as used by Tauler (cf. I, p. xlvi, n. 2), but in the sense of John 15:15: "I do not call you servants, . . . I call you friends" (Q). See also No. 9 (I, p. 79 and n. 2).

9. Cf. No. 8 (I, p. 75).

10. Elliptical in the original: either 'The more we are owned (by God), the less we own (our own selves)', or 'The more we own (ourselves), the less we are owned (by God)'. The meaning is much the same either way.

11. *De correptione et gratia* 24 (PL 44, 930) (Q).

12. The text is corrupt here. Q has 'And the more quickly they are hateful to him'; Clark: 'and all the more quickly if they are hateful to Him'.

13. Through revelation (Q).

14. Cf. No. 53 (II, p. 65) and No. 75 (II, p. 207).

15. The MSS erroneously have 'Paul' for 'John'.

16. *Nâchvolgenne* 'following' or 'imitation' as in the *Imitatio Christi* of Thomas à Kempis.

17. Cf. Appendix II.

18. Q puts a full stop after 'all things'. I follow Clark's punctuation.

19. Cf. No. 37 (I, p. 270).

20. Cf. No. 42 (I, p. 295) and No. 62 (II, p. 115).

21. Cf. n. 7 above.

22. Cf. No. 89 (II, p. 291). On the 'powers' see No. 1, n. 9 (I, p. 13).

23. Colledge (p. 273) mistranslates 'and that your trust is based on him' (*triuwe* modern *Treue* = 'loyalty').

24. On angels, see No. 31, n. 2 (I, p. 232); No. 95, n. 9 (II, p. 330).

25. Cf. No. 9 (I, p. 86).

26. Cf. No. 3 (I, p. 27).

27. 'und ie mêr wir des unsern *entwerden*, ie mêr wir in disem gewaerlîcher *werden*'. The play on words with *entwerden/werden* is hard to reproduce in English (but cf. No. 56 (II, p. 80)).

28. Clark's word for *entwerden* 'un-becoming'.

29. Cf. Thomas, *Summa Theol.* I, Q 1, A 1 and 2 (Q).

30. Cf. No. 97 (II, p. 340).
31. Pseudo-Dionysius (who was, of course, not a saint!): cf. *De mystica theol.*, ch. 1 (Q).
32. Diogenes.
33. Cf. 2 Cor. 12:2.

THE BOOK OF DIVINE COMFORT

Benedictus Deus et Pater Domini nostri Jesu Christi etc. (2 Cor. 1:3—4).

The noble apostle St Paul says this: "Blessed be God and the Father of our Lord Jesus Christ, the Father of mercies and God of all comfort, who comforts us in our tribulations". Three kinds of tribulation may beset a man and assail him in this land of exile. The first is misfortune occurring to outward goods; the second, to our relatives and dearest friends; the third, to ourselves: dishonour, hardship, pain of body and heart's distress.

Therefore I propose in this book to impart some teachings whereby a man may find consolation in all adversity, unhappiness and suffering. This book has three parts. In the first are to be found certain truths, from which may be deduced that which is well able, fully and fittingly, to comfort him in any trouble. After that he will find some thirty rules or maxims, in any one of which he will find full and sufficient solace. After that in the third part of this book he will find examples from the deeds and words done and spoken by wise people in times of tribulation.

I

In the first place, we should know that the wise man and wisdom, the true man and truth, the just man and justice, the good man and goodness are in correspondence and are

related to each other as follows: goodness is not created nor
made nor begotten, it is procreative and begets the good; and
the good man, in as far as he is good, is unmade and
uncreated, and yet the begotten child and son of goodness.[1]
Goodness begets itself and all that it is in the good man, and
the good man receives all his being, knowledge, love and
energy from the heart and inmost depth of goodness, and
from that alone. The good man and goodness are nothing but
one goodness, all in one, apart from the bearing and being
born, and yet the bearing of goodness and the being born in
the good man is but one being and one life. All that belongs
to the good man he gets from goodness and in goodness.
Therein he is and lives and dwells. There he knows himself
and all that he knows, and loves all that he loves, and works
with goodness in goodness, and goodness does all her works
with him and in him, just as it is written where the Son says:
"The Father remaining in me and dwelling in me performs
the works" (John 14:10), "The Father works until now and I
work" (John 5:17), "All that belongs to the Father is mine,
and all that is mine and pertains to mine is the Father's: His
in the giving and mine in the receiving" (John 17:10).

Further, we should know that when one says 'good', the
name or word denotes and includes nothing else, neither
more nor less than goodness pure and simple, which yet gives
itself out. When we speak of a good man, we mean that his
goodness has been given to him, infused, engendered by the
unborn goodness. Hence the gospel says: "As the Father has
life in Himself, so He has given to the Son to have the same
life in himself" (John 5:26). He says '*in* himself' not '*of*
himself', for the Father has given it to him.

All that I have said of the good man and goodness applies

equally to the true man and truth, to the just man and justice, to the wise man and wisdom, to God's Son and God the Father, to every God-begotten thing that has no father on earth, in which, too, nothing is born that is created which is not God, in which there is no image but God alone, naked and pure. For this is what St John says in his gospel: "To all of them is given power and strength to become sons of God, who were not born of blood nor of the will of the flesh or of the will of man, but of God and from God alone" (John 1:12f.). By the blood he means everything in man not subordinate to the human will. By the will of the flesh he means whatever in a man is subject to his will, but with resistance and reluctance, which inclines to the carnal appetites and is common to the body and the soul, not peculiar to the soul alone, in consequence of which the soul's powers become tired, feeble and old. By the will of man St John means the highest powers of the soul,[2] whose nature and work is unmixed with flesh, which reside in the pure nature of the soul, detached from time and space and from all that has any hankering or taste for the things of time and space, having noting in common with anything, in which man is formed in the image of God, in which man is of God's lineage and God's kindred. And yet, since they are not God Himself but are in the soul and created with the soul, therefore they must lose their form and be transformed into God and be born in God and from God, with only God for Father, for thus they too become God's sons and God's only-begotten Son. For I am the son of all that which forms me after its own image and in itself, and bears me thus. Such a man, God's son, good the son of goodness, just the son of justice, in so far as he is her son, she (justice) is unborn-bearing, and her born son has the same single being as justice has and is, and is possessed of all that pertains to justice and truth.

From all this teaching, which is found in the holy gospel and is clearly grasped in the natural light of the rational soul,[3] there is true solace for every human sorrow. St Augustine says: 'For God nothing is far or long'.[4] If you wish for nothing to be far away or long for you, then conform to God, for then a thousand years are as one day — today. Thus I say that in God there is no sorrow or suffering or distress. If you would be free from all adversity and pain, turn and cleave entirely to God. Assuredly, all your ills are because you do not turn to God and God alone. If you were formed and begotten into righteousness alone, in truth nothing could pain you, any more than righteousness can pain God. Solomon says: "The just will not grieve, whatever may befall" (Prov. 12:21). He does not say the just man or the just angel or this or that: he says 'the just'.[5] Whatever appertains to the just, especially the fact that justice is his and he is just, all *that* is a 'son', and has a father on earth and is a creature, made and created, for its father is a creature, made and created. But 'the just' pure and simple, since this has no made or created father, and God and justice are one, and justice alone is its father, therefore pain and sorrow cannot enter into him any more than into God. Justice cannot sadden him, for all joy, delight and bliss are justice; thus if justice grieved the just it would be grieving itself. No iniquity or injustice, nothing made or created can grieve the just, for everything created is as far beneath him as it is beneath God, it makes no impression or influence on the just, and is not begotten in him whose father is God alone. Therefore a man should strive earnestly to de-form himself of himself and of all creatures, and know no father but God alone. Then nothing will be able to afflict or sadden him, neither God nor creature, created or uncreated, and all his being, life, knowledge, wisdom and love will be from God and in God, and *be* God.

Another thing one should know that will console a man in any tribulation. It is that the just and good man assuredly delights immeasurably, unspeakably more in doing right than he or even the highest angel delights and rejoices in his natural being and life. That is why the saints gladly gave their lives for justice.

I say then: when outward ills befall the good and just man, if he remains in equanimity with the peace of his heart unmoved, then it is true, as I have said, that nothing that happens to him can disturb the just.[6] But if he is perturbed by outward mishaps, then truly it is right and proper that God has permitted him to suffer this harm, for he wanted and thought to be just and yet was upset by so small a thing.[7] If it is right for God, then indeed he should not be grieved thereby but should rejoice for it far more than for his own life, which a man rejoices in and values more than all this world; for what would this world profit a man if he were not?

The third thing we can and should know is that, according to natural truth, God alone is the sole fount and vein of all goodness, essential truth and comfort, and whatever is not God has of itself a natural bitterness, discomfort and unhappiness, and adds nothing to the goodness which is from God and is God, but rather lessens, dims and hides the sweetness, joy and comfort that God gives.

And further I declare that all sorrow comes from love of that which loss has deprived me of. If I mind the loss of outward things, it is a sure sign that I am fond of outward things, and *really* love sorrow and discomfort! Is it to be wondered at, then, that I am grieved, if I love and seek sorrow and discomfort? My heart and inclination ascribe to creatures what belongs to God. I turn to creatures, whence by nature discomfort comes, and turn away from God, from whom all comfort flows. Is it to be wondered at that I am sad and grieved? For indeed, in very truth it is impossible for God or the whole world to give solace to one who looks for it in creatures. But he who should love God alone in creatures and creatures in God alone, *he* would find true, real and equal comfort everywhere. Let this suffice for the first part of this book.

II

Now, in the second part, there follow some thirty grounds, any one of which alone should suffice to comfort the rational man in his trouble.

The first is that no hardship or loss is without some comfort, and no loss is total loss. That is why St Paul says that God's good faith and goodness does not permit any trial or tribulation to be insupportable.[8] He always makes and gives some consolation with which a man can find help. For the saints and the pagan masters also say that God and nature cannot brook the existence of undiluted evil or suffering.[9]

Let us suppose a man has a hundred marks, of which he loses forty and keeps sixty. If he goes on brooding over the forty he has lost, he must remain disconsolate and woeful. How can he take comfort and be free from care, if he turns towards the loss and tribulation, impressing it upon himself and himself upon it, so that he looks at it and it looks back at him, and he talks and converses with the loss and the loss converses with him, and they gaze at each other face to face? But if he would but turn to the sixty marks he still has and turn his back on the forty that are lost, and reflect on the sixty and gaze at *them* face to face, then he would assuredly be consoled. What exists, is good and can comfort us, but what is naught and is no good, what is not mine and is lost to me, can only bring disappointment, woe and distress. Accordingly Solomon says: "In the days of adversity do not forget the days of prosperity" (cf. Eccl. 11:27). That is to say, if you are in woe and distress, think of the profit and ease that you still have and hold. There is comfort too in the thought of how many thousands there are who, if they had the sixty marks you still possess, would think themselves lords and ladies and wealthy, and would rejoice in their hearts.

There is something else that should comfort you. If a man is sick and in great bodily pain, but he has his home and all his needs in the way of food and drink and medical aid, and servants to nurse him, the sympathy and companionship of his friends, what should he do? What do poor folk do who have just as much or greater sickness and hardship and none to give them a cup of cold water? They must beg for a bare crust in the rain, cold and snow from house to house. So, if you would be comforted, forget those who are better off and just remember those who are worse off than you.

Further, I declare, all suffering comes from love and attachment. So if I suffer on account of transitory things, then I and my heart have love and attachment for temporal things, I do not love God with all my heart and do not yet love that which God wishes me to love with Him. Is it any wonder then that God permits me to be rightly afflicted with loss and sorrow?

St Augustine says: 'Lord, I did not want to lose thee, but in my greed I wanted to have creatures besides thee; therefore I have lost thee, for thou wouldst not have man possess the falsehood and deceit of creatures alongside thee, who art truth'. [10] And elsewhere he says that he is altogether too greedy who is not content with God alone. And again he says: 'How should God's gifts to creatures satisfy a man who is not satisfied with God Himself?' [11] To a good man that should be no comfort but pain which is alien to God, unlike Him and not God Himself alone. He should always say: 'Lord God my comfort, if thou sendest me away from thee to anything else, then give me another thee, that I may go from thee to thee, for I want nothing but thee.' [12] When the Lord promised Moses all blessings and sent him into the Holy Land, which denotes heaven, Moses said: "Lord, send me nowhere but where thou wilt accompany me" (cf. Ex. 33:15).

All inclination, desire and affection comes from likeness, for all things tend towards and love their likes. [13] The pure man loves purity, the just man loves and inclines to justice; a man's lips speak of what is within, just as our Lord says: "Out of the fullness of the heart the mouth speaks" (Luke 6:45), and Solomon says: "All the labour of a man is in his mouth" (Eccl. 6:7). Thus it is a sure sign that not God but creature is in a man's heart if he finds attachment and consolation without. And therefore a virtuous man should be very ashamed before God, and in his own eyes, if he becomes aware that God is not in him, and God the Father is not active in him, but that the wretched creature is still living and yearning in him and acting in him. Accordingly King David says and laments in the Psalms: "Tears have been my comfort day and night, as long as they could say to me, Where is your

God?" (Ps. 42:3 [AV]). To turn to outward things and to find comfort in what is comfortless, and to speak eagerly and overmuch about it — that is a true sign that God is not apparent in me, is not watching and working in me. Still more should he be ashamed for good people to be aware of this in him. The good man should never rail at loss or sorrow: he should only lament that he *does* lament them, and that he is aware of his own wailing and lamentation.

The masters say that under heaven there is fire, widespread and fierce and with nothing in between, and yet heaven is not in the least affected by it. [14] One writer says that the lowest part of the soul is nobler than the summit of heaven. [15] How then can a man claim to be a celestial being whose heart is in heaven, if he is distressed and troubled by such trivial things?

Now I will turn to another matter. A man cannot be good who does not wish for exactly what God wills, for it is impossible that God should will anything but good, and precisely in and because God wills it, it must be good and best. That is why our Lord taught the apostles, and us through them, to pray every day that God's will be done. And yet, when God's will appears and is done, we complain.

Seneca, a pagan master, asks: 'What is the best comfort in suffering and distress?', and says it is that a man should take all things as if he had wished and prayed for them: for you *would* have wished it had you realised that all things come about from, with and in God's will. [16] A pagan master declared: 'Ruler, supreme Father and Lord of the highest heaven, all that you will I am prepared for. Vouchsafe me the will to live according to your will.' [17]

A good man should trust in God, believe and be assured that God is so good that it is impossible for God, His goodness and love to endure that any pain or suffering befall a man unless either to save that man from further suffering, or else to give him greater consolation on earth, or to make thereby and therefrom something better which should redound more largely and fully to God's glory. Yet be that as it may: by the mere fact of its being God's will that it should occur, the good man's will should be so much at one and united with God's will, that that man would will the same as God, even though it were to his own harm or indeed his damnation. Thus St Paul wished to be sundered from God for God's sake and to the glory of God (cf. Rom. 9:3). [18] For the truly perfected man should be wont to be so dead to self, so lost in God to his own form and so transformed in God's will, that his entire blessedness consists in unknowing of himself and all things, and knowing only God, willing nothing and knowing no will but God's will, willing to know God, as St Paul says, "as God knows me" (cf. 1 Cor. 13:12). God knows all that he knows, loves and wills all that he wills, in Himself and in His own will. Our Lord says: "That is eternal life, to know God alone" (John 17:3).

Therefore the masters declare that the blessed in heaven know creatures independently of any image of those creatures, knowing them in the one image that is God, in which God knows Himself and all things, and loves and wills them. And God Himself teaches us to pray for and desire this, when we say "Our Father", "hallowed be thy name" — that is, to know You alone — "thy kingdom come", that I may possess nothing I prize and regard as wealth but You, who are all riches. Therefore the gospel says: "Blessed are the poor in spirit" (Matt. 5:3), that is, in *will*, and so we pray to God that His will may be done "in earth" (that is, in ourselves) and "in heaven" (that is, in God Himself). Such a man is so one-willed with God that he wills all that God wills and in the way God wills it. And so, since God in a way wills that I should have sinned, I would not wish that I had not done so, [19] for thus God's will is done "in earth" (that is, in ill-doing) as well as "in heaven" (that is, in well-doing). In this way one wills to do without God for God's sake, to be sundered from God for God's sake, and that alone is true repentance for my sins: then I grieve for sin without grief, as God grieves for all evil without grief. I have grief, the greatest grief, for my sins, for I would not sin for everything that is created or creaturely, even though there were a thousand worlds existing to all eternity — and yet without grief; and I accept and take the suffering in God's will and from God's will. *Such* suffering alone is perfect suffering, for it arises and springs from pure love of God's sheer goodness and joy. Thus it is made true, and one comes to know it, as I have said in this little book, that the good man, in so far as he is good, enters into full possession of that goodness which God is in Himself.

Now observe what an amazing and blissful life this man must lead "in earth as in heaven" — in God Himself! Discomfort serves him as comfort, grief as well as joy — and note too the special comfort it brings: for, if I have the grace and goodness of which I have spoken, then I am at all times and in all ways equally comforted and happy; and if I lack it, then I shall do without it for God's sake and by God's will. If God wills to give me what I want, then I have it and have the pleasure of it; if God does not will to give it to me, then I get it by doing without, in God's same will, and thus I take by doing without and not taking. So what do I lose? Really and truly, one receives God in a truer sense by doing without than by getting, for when a man gets something, it is the gift itself which is the cause of his being happy and comforted. But if he receives nothing, he has, finds and knows nothing to rejoice at but God, and God's will alone.

There is yet another comfort. If a man has lost his outward goods, a friend or a kinsman, an eye, a hand, or whatever it may be, then, if he endures it patiently for God's sake, he can be sure at least of having before God all that for which he would not have wished to bear it.[20] If a man loses an eye, and if he would not have sacrificed his eye for a thousand marks, or for six thousand marks or more — then assuredly he has before God, and in God, all the amount that he would have given in order not to endure such loss or pain. This is perhaps what was meant when our Lord said: "It is better for you to enter into eternal life with one eye than to be lost with two" (Matt. 18:9). It may also be the meaning of God's words: "He who leaves father and mother and sister and brother, farm and fields or anything else, shall receive a hundredfold *and* eternal life" (Matt. 19:29; Mark 10:29–30). For a certainty, I can say this in God's truth and by my salvation, that whoever for God's sake and for goodness leaves father and mother, brother and sister or whatever it may be, receives a hundredfold in double fashion: firstly, that his father and mother, brother and sister, become a hundred times dearer to him than they are now; and in another way, that not just a hundred, but all people, inasmuch as they are people and human, become far dearer to him than his father, mother or brother are to him now by nature. If a man cannot understand this, it is purely and solely because he has not yet, for God's sake and for goodness, totally renounced father and mother, sister and brother and all things. *How* has a man abandoned father and mother, sister and brother for God's sake, if he has them still on earth in his heart, if he is still sad, and considers and regards what is not God? How has he abandoned all things for God's sake, who still considers and regards this or that good? St Augustine says: 'Remove this and that good, then pure goodness remains hovering in its simple extent: that is God'.[21] For, as I have said above, this and that good adds nothing to goodness, rather it hides and covers up the goodness in us. He knows and sees this who sees and perceives in truth, for it is true in truth, and therefore one must perceive it there[22] and nowhere else.

But we should know that there is a difference of degree in the possession of virtue and the will to suffer, just as we see in nature that one man is bigger and fairer in form, in complexion, in knowledge and skills than another. And so I say that a good man can be truly good and yet be moved and shaken, to a greater or lesser extent, by natural love of father, mother, sister and brother without falling away from God or from goodness. Yet he is good, or better, according as he is less or more comforted and moved by the natural love and inclination for father, mother, sister and brother, and for himself, and is aware of this.

And yet, as I have written above, if a man could accept this in God's will, inasmuch as it is God's will that man's nature has such shortcomings precisely because of God's justice in regard to the sin of the first man, and if he were equally willing to do without if, in God's will, things were otherwise, then all would be well with him and he would find assured consolation in his suffering. This is the sense of St John's words that the true "light shines in the darkness" (John 1:5), and of what St Paul says, that virtue is perfected in weakness (2 Cor. 12:9). If a thief could truly, fully, purely, gladly, willingly and happily suffer death for love of divine justice, in which and according to which God wills in His justice that the evil-doer be slain, he would assuredly be saved and blessed.

Yet another comfort is this: probably no one can be found who is not fond enough of some living being to gladly do without an eye or be blind for a year, if at the end of it he could have his sight again and if he could thus save his friend from death. Now if a man is ready to sacrifice his eye to save another from death, who in any case is bound to die in a few years' time, surely he should be the more ready to give the ten, twenty or thirty years he may still have to live to gain his eternal happiness, and to see God eternally in His divine light, and himself and all creatures in God.

A further consolation: a good man, in so far as he is good, born of goodness alone and an image of goodness, considers all that is created as *this* or *that* to be unpleasing, bitter and harmful. The reason? Because the loss of *that* is release, the loss of pain, discomfort and harm. In truth, to lose one's sorrow is true comfort. So a man should not lament his loss. He should rather lament that comfort is unknown to him, that comfort cannot comfort him, as a sick man cannot savour the sweetness of wine. He should lament, as I have written before, that he is not fully de-formed of creatures and is not totally in-formed in goodness.

A man should also remember in his trouble that God speaks truth and promises by Himself, the Truth. If God were to break His word He would lapse from His Godhead and would not be God, for He is His word, His truth. His word is that our sorrow shall be turned to joy (Jeremiah

3:31; John 16:20). Truly, if I knew that all my stones were to be transformed into gold, then the more and the bigger the stones I had, the happier I should be; I should ask for stones and collect them, big ones in plenty; the more they were and the bigger, the better I should like them. In this way a man would be powerfully comforted in tribulation.

Another of the same kind: no vessel can hold two separate kinds of drink. If it is to contain wine, we must pour out the water; the vessel must be bare and empty. And so, if you would receive divine joy and God, you must pour away creatures.[23] St Augustine says: 'Pour out, that you may be filled. Learn not to love that you may learn to love. Turn away that you may be turned towards.'[24] In short, to take in, to be receptive, a thing must be empty. The masters say that if the eye had any colour in it in perceiving, it would perceive neither the colour it had nor those it had not. But since it is free of all colour, it perceives all colours.[25] The wall has colour in it, and so perceives neither its own colour nor any other, it cares naught for colour, no more for gold and azure than for coal-black. The eye has no colour, and yet truly has it, for it rejoices in colour with pleasure and delight. And the more perfect and pure the powers of the soul are, the more perfectly and extensively they take in what they perceive, and receive the more widely and have the greater delight in, and become the more one with what they receive, so much so that the highest power of the soul, which is bare of all things and has nothing in common with things, receives nothing less than God Himself in the extent and fullness of His being.[26] And the masters show that nothing can equal this union, this fusion and bliss for joy and delight.[27] Therefore our Lord says in striking words: "Blessed are the poor in spirit" (Matt.

5:3). He is poor who has nothing. "Poor in spirit" means: as the eye is 'poor' and bare of colour yet receptive of all colours, so is he poor in spirit who is receptive of all spirit, and the spirit of all spirits is God. The fruit of the spirit is love, joy and peace.[28] Bareness, and poverty, having nothing and being empty transforms nature; emptiness makes water run upwards and performs many other miracles of which it is not the place to speak now.

So, if you would seek and find perfect joy and comfort in God, see to it that you are free of all creatures and of all comfort from creatures; for assuredly, as long as you are or can be comforted by creatures, you will never find true comfort. But when nothing can comfort you but God, then God *will* comfort you, and with Him and in Him all that is bliss. While what is not God comforts you, you will have no comfort here or hereafter, but when creatures give you no comfort and you have no taste for them, *then* you will find comfort both here and hereafter.

If a man might and knew how to make a cup completely empty and keep it empty of whatever might fill it, even air, assuredly that cup would lose and forget its own nature, and emptiness would bear it aloft.[29] So too, being bare, poor and void of all creatures carries the soul to God. Likeness, too, and heat are causes of ascent. Likeness we ascribe to the Son in the Godhead, heat and love to the Holy Ghost. Likeness in all things, more especially and firstly in the divine nature, is the birth of the one, and likeness of one, in one and with one is the origin and source of the flowering, ardent love. One is beginning without any beginning.[30] Likeness is beginning begotten of the One alone, getting its being, and its being-a-beginning, from and in the One. It is the nature of love to arise and flow out of two as a one. One as one is not love; two as two is not love; but two as one must needs produce natural, willing, ardent love.

Now Solomon says that all waters (that is all creatures) flow back and return to their source (Eccl. 1:7). Therefore it must be true, as I have said: likeness and ardent love raise, lead and convey the soul into the prime source of the one, that is, the Father of all things in heaven and earth (cf. Ephes. 4:6). I therefore say that likeness, born of one, draws the soul to God, just as He is in His hidden unity, for that is the meaning of 'one'. We have a visible symbol of this: when material fire burns wood, a spark receives the nature of the fire and becomes like that pure fire which exists immediately below heaven.[31] All at once it forgets and renounces father and mother, brother and sister on earth and shoots up to its heavenly father.[32] The father of the spark, here below, is the fire, its mother is the wood, its brother and sister are the other sparks, and for these the first spark will not wait. It shoots up quickly to its true father, who is heaven; for whoever knows the truth knows well that the fire, as fire, is not a real, true father of the spark. The real, true father of the spark and all that is fiery is heaven. Further, it is important to note that this little spark not only leaves and forgets father and mother, brother and sister on earth; it also leaves and forgets and abandons itself in its urgent desire to get to its true father, heaven, for it is bound to be quenched by the cold air; and yet it wants to give proof of the natural love it bears for its real, heavenly father.

And just as I have said above concerning emptiness or purity that, in proportion as the soul is more perfect, bare and poor and has less of creatures, and is more free of all things that are not God, so she receives God more purely and more in God, becomes more one with God and looks into God and God into her, as in an image transfigured, as St Paul says (2 Cor. 3:18), even so I declare in regard to likeness and the ardour of love: for the more anything is *like* another, the more it rushes to that other, the quicker it moves and the sweeter and more joyous its progression; and the further it leaves behind itself, and whatever is not the other, the more it becomes like that towards which it is hurrying. And since likeness flows from the One, drawing and attracting by dint of and in virtue of the One, so there is no stilling or satisfying either that which draws, or that which is drawn, till they are united in the One. Therefore our Lord speaks through the prophet Isaiah to the effect that no high likeness and no peace of love satisfies me, until I myself appear in my Son, and I myself am kindled and set ablaze in the love of the Holy Ghost (cf. Is. 62:1). [33] And our Lord besought his Father that we should become one with Him and in Him, not merely united (cf. John 17:11). We have a clear image and demonstration of this saying and this truth in nature, even outwardly: when fire is at work kindling and burning wood, the fire makes the wood quite small and unlike its former self, robbing it of solidity, cold, mass and moisture, and making the wood more and more like itself, the fire; and yet neither fire nor wood is stilled or quieted or sated by any warmth or heat or likeness, till the fire gives birth to itself in the wood and gives it its own nature and also its own being, so that all is one fire, of like property, undifferentiated, neither more nor less. And so, until this comes about there is always a reeking, fighting, crackling, toil and strife between the fire and the wood. But when all unlikeness has been abolished and cast out, the fire dies down and the wood is silent. Further I declare in truth that the hidden power of nature abhors hidden likeness in so far as it bears within itself some difference and duality, seeking in it the *one*, loving this in it and for its sake alone,[34] just as the mouth seeks in and from the wine only the taste or the sweetness, loving only this. If water had the same taste as wine, the mouth would relish wine no more than water.

That is why I have said that the soul hates and has no love for likeness, for likeness in and for itself, but she loves it for the One that is concealed in it and is the true Father, a beginningless beginning of all that is in heaven and earth. And so I say that as long as likeness is found and appears between fire and wood, there is no true joy or peace there, no rest, no satisfaction. Therefore the masters say that the generation of fire comes through conflict, pain and unrest, and in time. But the birth of the fire and the joy are beyond time and space. Joy and pleasure never seem too long or too far. All that I have said is intended by our Lord's words: "A woman giving birth to a child endures sorrow, pain and suffering, but when the child is born, she forgets the pain and woe" (John 16:20). Therefore God speaks to us in the gospel and reminds us to pray the heavenly Father that our joy may be perfect (John 15:11), and St Philip said: "Lord, show us the Father, and it will suffice us" (John 14:8); for 'father' means birth and not likeness, it means the One, in which likeness is silent and everything is stilled that desires being.

Now a man can see quite clearly why and how he lacks consolation in all his pain, adversity and loss. This comes wholly and solely from the fact that he is remote from God and not free of creatures, unlike to God and cold in divine love.

But there is another reason, observing and knowing which a man would rightly be comforted in outward loss and sorrow. Suppose a man goes a certain way or starts on one task, leaving another, and then he suffers harm: he breaks a leg or an arm, or loses an eye or falls ill. If he keeps on thinking, 'if only I[35] had taken a different road or done something different, this would never have happened', he will remain disconsolate and is bound to suffer. And so he should think, 'if I had gone a different way, or done or not done something else, I might well have suffered some far greater loss or harm', and then he will be comforted.

Here is another point. If you have lost a thousand marks, do not bewail the thousand marks you have lost. You should thank God who gave you the thousand marks to lose, and who grants you the chance, by practising the virtue of patience, to gain eternal life, which many thousands have not.

And here is another comforting reflection. Suppose a man has had honour and comfort for many years, and now loses all this by God's decree. That man should reflect wisely and thank God. When he realises the loss and tribulation he now has, then for the first time he will understand what profit and security he had before, and should thank God for the security he enjoyed without appreciating it, and not be angry. He ought to realise that a man gets by nature nothing by himself but ill and imperfection. Whatever is good or goodness, God has lent, not given him. For whoever knows the truth knows that God, the heavenly Father, gives the Son and the Holy Ghost all that is good; but to creatures He *gives* nothing good, but only lends it. The sun gives heat to the air, but the light is loaned, and so, as soon as the sun sets, the air loses the light, but retains the heat, for this is given to it for its own.[36] Therefore the masters say that God, the heavenly Father, is the father, not the lord of the Son, nor the lord of the Holy Ghost. But God-Father, Son and Holy Ghost is one lord and lord of creatures, and we say that God is eternally Father, but from when He created creatures He has been Lord.[37]

Now I say, since whatever is good or comforting or temporal is only lent to a man, what right has he to complain when the lender wishes to take it back? He should thank God, who lent it to him for so long. He should even thank Him for not taking back all that He has lent; for it would be only just if God took back all that He had lent when a man was angry at a part being taken away, which was never his, and of which he never was the master. Accordingly, the prophet Jeremiah spoke well, in the throes of pain and lamentation, when he said: "Oh how great and manifold are God's mercies, that we are not destroyed!" (Lam. 3:22). If a man had lent me his jacket, fur-coat and cloak, and if he were to take back the cloak, leaving me the jacket and fur-coat in the frost, I should thank him heartily and be glad. You should specially note how badly I am in the wrong if I rage and lament whenever I lose something; for if I want the good thing that I have to be given to me and not merely lent, that means I want to be a lord and God's natural son, and perfect, although I am not yet even God's son by grace — for it is a quality of the Son of God, and of the Holy Ghost, to be equable under all conditions.

Further, we should know that the natural human virtues are without doubt of such nobility and power that no outward work is too hard for them, nor indeed big enough for them to find full scope in it or at it, or to find (adequate) expression. And therefore there is an inner work which neither time nor space can enclose or contain. In it is that which is divine and in it is that which is divine and like God, whom neither time nor space encloses — for He is everywhere and equally present at all times — and it is also like God in this respect, that no creature can fully embrace Him or mirror God's goodness in itself. Therefore there must be something more inward, more exalted and uncreated, something without measure or mode in which the heavenly Father may properly imprint, pour forth and manifest Himself, that is to say the Son and the Holy Ghost.

And none can hinder this work of virtue, any more than one can hinder God. Day and night this work glistens and shines. It glorifies God and sings His praise in a new song, just as David says: "Sing unto the Lord a new song" (Ps. 96:1 [AV]). *His* praise is earthly, and God does not love that work which is outward, confined to time and space, which is narrow and subject to hindrance and constraint, which tires and grows old with time and use. The (inner) work is loving God, intending good and goodness, in which whatever a man wills and *would* have done with a pure and total will in all good works, he has *already done*, being in this respect like God, of whom David says: "All that He has intended, He has already done and performed" (Ps. 135:6 [AV]).

We have a clear illustration of this teaching in a stone. Its outward work consists in falling down and lying on the ground. This work may be hindered, for it is not falling all the time without interruption. But there is another work more inward in the stone, and that is a downward tendency,

82

which is inherent in it;[38] neither God nor creature nor anyone can stop this. The stone performs this work day and night without a break. It might lie up above for a thousand years, and yet its tendency to fall would be no greater and no less than on the first day. In the same way I say of virtue that she has an inner work: a will and tendency towards all good, and a flight from and a repugnance to all that is bad, evil and incompatible with God and goodness. And the worse an act is, and the less godly, the stronger the repugnance; and the greater the work and the more godlike, the easier, more welcome and pleasanter it is to her. And her sole complaint and sorrow — if she could feel sorrow — is that this suffering for God is too little, and all outward, temporal works are too little for her to be able to find full expression, realisation and shape in them.[39] By practice she becomes strong, and by giving she becomes rich. She does not wish to have suffered and to have got over pain and suffering: she is willing and eager to suffer always without ceasing for God and well-doing. All her happiness lies in suffering, and not in *having suffered*, for God's sake. And therefore our Lord says quite deliberately: "Blessed are those who suffer for righteousness' sake" (Matt. 5:10): he does not say 'who have suffered'. Such a man hates 'having suffered', for 'having suffered' is not the suffering that he loves. And so I say too that such a man hates 'going to suffer', for that too is not suffering. Yet he hates 'going to suffer' less than 'having suffered', for 'having suffered' is further from suffering and more unlike it, being over and done with. But suffering to come does not take away all suffering which he loves.

St Paul says that he would choose to be separated from God that God's glory might be enhanced (Rom. 9:3).[40] They say these words were spoken by St Paul when he was not yet perfected. But I think this was the utterance of a perfect heart. It is also said that he meant that he only wanted to be separated from God for a time. But I say that a perfect man would be as loath to be apart from God for a single hour as for a thousand years. Yet, if it were God's will and to God's glory that he should be deprived of God, then a thousand years, or even eternity, would be as easy to him as a day or a single hour.

The inner world, too, is godly, divine and endowed with the character of God so that, just as all creatures — though there were a thousand worlds — are not one hair's breadth better than God alone, so I declare and have said before, that this outer work cannot add either by quantity or size, nor by length or breadth nor in any other way to the value of the inner work, whose value lies in itself. And so the outer work can never be small if the inner work is great, neither can the outer be great or good if the inner is little or nothing. The inner work contains in itself all time, all magnitude, all breadth and length. The inner work draws and derives its entire being only from God and in God's heart; it receives the Son and is born as the Son in the heavenly Father's womb. With the outward work it is not so: this gets its divine goodness through the channel of the inner work, produced and poured out in a downflowing from the Godhead that is clothed with distinction, quantity, part, all of which and the like of which, even likeness itself, is far from God and alien to Him. [41] These all cling and cleave to, and rest in that which is good, which is illumined, which is creaturely, blind altogether to goodness and light in themselves, and to the One wherein God bears His only-begotten Son, and in him

all who are God's children, born sons. [42] There is the fount and
origin of the Holy Ghost from whom alone, as he is the spirit
of God and God Himself is a spirit, the spirit is begotten in
us. It flows forth from all who are God's sons, according as
they are in greater or lesser degree born purely of God alone,
in God's image, transformed in God and estranged from all
multiplicity (such as is still to be found according to their
nature in even the highest angels), estranged indeed even (for
him who can grasp this!) from goodness, from truth, and
from anything at all which even in thought or name permits
the merest hint or shadow of difference; and is entrusted to
the One, bare of all number and variety, [43] wherein one
God-Father-Son-and-Holy-Ghost loses and is stripped of all
distinctions and properties, and is One alone. And that One
makes us blessed, and the further we are from this One, the
less we are sons and Son, and the less perfectly the Holy Ghost
wells up in us and flows from us. That is what our Lord,
God's Son in the Godhead, meant by saying: "Whoever
drinks from the water that I give, in him a fountain of water
shall arise, springing up to everlasting life" (John 4:14). And
St John says he was speaking of the Holy Ghost (John 7:39).
The Son in the Godhead gives by his own nature nothing but
sonship, God-begottenness, the fountain, origin and out-
flowing of the Holy Ghost, of the love of God, the full, true
and perfect savour of the One, the Heavenly Father. Therefore the Father's voice speaks from heaven to the Son: "You
are my beloved Son, in whom I am beloved and well pleased"
(Matt. 3:17), for without a doubt, no one loves God in
fullness and purity who is not God's son. For love, the Holy
Ghost, arises in and issues from the Son, and the Son loves the
Father for His own sake, the Father in himself and himself in

the Father. Therefore our Lord says so truly: "Blessed are the poor in spirit" (Matt. 5:3), that is, those who have nothing of their own, human spirit, and come naked to God. And St Paul says: "God has revealed it to us in His spirit" (1 Cor. 2:10).

St Augustine says that man will understand the scriptures best of all who is bare of spirit and seeks the sense and truth of scripture itself, in the same spirit in which it is written or spoken: in God's spirit. [44] St Peter says that all holy men have spoken in the spirit of God (2 Peter 1:21). St Paul says: "No man can tell and know what is in man but the spirit that is in man, and none can tell what is the spirit of God and in God but the spirit that is of God and is God" (1 Cor. 2:11). Thus a certain writing, a gloss, [45] says truly that none can understand or teach the Pauline writings unless he has the same spirit in which St Paul spoke and wrote. And that is always my sole complaint, that vulgar people, who lack God's spirit and have it not, seek to judge according to their crude human sense what they hear or read about in scripture, which is spoken and written in and by the Holy Spirit, not considering that it is written: "What is impossible for men is possible for God" (Matt. 19:26). And indeed it is common in the natural sphere, that what is impossible to the lower nature is usual and natural to the higher.

From this you should also deduce what I have just said, that a good man, God's son born in God, loves God for His own sake, in Himself, and many other things I have previously declared. To understand it better one should know, as I have also said before, that a good man, born of goodness and in God, enters into all the qualities of the divine nature. Now God has one property according to

Solomon, that everything is wrought by God for His own sake (Prov. 16:4), that is to say that He does not pay regard to any 'why' or 'wherefore' outside of Himself, other than for His own sake; He loves and does all things for Himself. So, if a man loves God for Himself and all things, and does all his deeds not for reward, for honour or for pleasure, but for God and God's glory alone, that is a sign that he is God's son.

Still further, God loves for His own sake and performs all things for His own sake alone, that is, He loves for love's sake and works for the sake of working, for indeed, God would never have begotten His only-begotten Son in eternity if 'being begotten' were not the same as 'begetting'. Therefore the saints declare that the Son has been begotten eternally in that he is still being begotten unceasingly.[46] Nor would God have ever created the world if being created were not creation. And so — God *has* created the world by still continually creating it. Whatever is past or future is alien to and remote from God. And therefore, whoever is born of God as God's son, loves God for God's sake, that is, he loves for the sake of loving God and acts for the sake of acting. God never tires of loving and working, and whatever He loves is *one* love. Therefore it is true that God is love. And that is why I said above that the good man always wants and desires to suffer for God's sake, not to *have* suffered: in suffering he has that which he loves. He loves to suffer for God's sake, and he suffers for God's sake. Therefore and therein a man is God's son, formed after God and in God, who loves for his own sake, that is, he loves for the sake of loving, works for the sake of working; and for that reason God loves and works without ceasing. And God's work is His nature, His being, His life and His felicity. Thus in very truth, for the son of God, for a good man is so far as he is God's son, suffering for God's sake, working for God is his being, his life, his work, his felicity, for our Lord declares: "Blessed are they that suffer for righteousness' sake" (Matt. 5:10).

Again, in the third place, I declare that a good man, so far as he is good, has God's nature not only in loving all he loves and doing all he does for the sake of God whom he loves therein and for whom he works, but he loves and works also for himself, for Him who loves; for what he loves is God-Father-Unborn, and He who loves is God-Son-Born. Now the Father is in the Son and the Son in the Father. Father and Son are One.[47] Concerning how the most inward or highest part of the soul draws and receives God's Son and becomes God's Son in the heavenly Father's womb and heart, look at the end of this book, where I have written "Of the Nobleman who went into a distant country to gain a kingdom for himself, and returned" (Luke 19:12).

One should also know that in nature the impress and inflow of the highest and supreme nature is more delightful and pleasing to anything than its own nature and essence. Water flows downwards of its own nature, and its being resides in that.[48] Yet through the impress and influence of the moon up in the sky, it abandons and forgets its own nature, flowing upstream and upwards, and this effluxion is easier for it than the downflow. From this a man may know whether it would be right for him, if it would be pleasant and delightful for him to abandon his natural will, to give it up and to deny himself totally in everything that God wants him to suffer. And that is the true meaning of our Lord's words: "Whoever will come to me, let him go out of himself and deny himself and take up his cross"[49] (Matt. 16:24), that is, he shall lay aside whatever is cross and suffering. For assuredly, whoever had abandoned self and completely gone forth from self, for him nothing could be a cross or pain or suffering: it would all be a joy, a pleasure and heart's delight, and that man would come and truly follow God. For just as nothing can make God sad or sorrowful, so nothing could make him sad or sorry. And so, when our Lord says: "Whoever will come to me, let him go out of himself and deny himself and take up his cross and follow me", this is not merely a commandment, as is commonly said and thought: it is a promise and a divine prescription for a man to make all his suffering, all his deeds and all his life happy and joyful. It is more a reward than a commandment.[50] For a man who is in that state has whatever he wants, and wants nothing evil, and that is blessedness. Therefore again our Lord says: "Blessed are they that suffer for righteousness' sake".

Again, our Lord's words, "Let him deny himself and take up his cross and come to me" mean: become a son as I am Son, born-God and the same One that I am, that I draw in, indwelling, abiding within the Father's bosom and heart. "Father", says the Son, "I will that my follower, he that comes to me, shall be where I am" (John 12:26). No one comes more truly to the Son, as he is Son, than he who becomes a son, and no one is where the Son is (who is the Father's bosom and heart, One in One), than he who is a son. "I", says the Father, "will lead her into the wilderness and speak to her heart" (Hosea 2:14). Heart to heart, one in one is how God loves. Whatever is other and different from that, God hates. God entices and lures to the One. All creatures, even the lowest, seek the One, and the highest perceive the One. Caught up above nature and transformed, they seek

One in One, One in Itself. That may well be what the Son means to say: 'In the Son of the Godhead, in the Father, where I am shall he be who serves me, who follows me, who comes to me.'[51]

There is a further consolation. You should know that it is impossible for all nature to break, destroy or even touch anything without intending betterment for that which is touched.[52] Not content with doing equal good, she always wants to do something better. How is that? A wise physician never touches a man's bad finger so as to hurt him unless he can make the finger better, or make the man generally better, or give him relief. If he can make the man or the finger better, he does so. If he cannot, he cuts off the finger to benefit the man. And it is much better to lose the finger and save the man than to let both perish. One loss is preferable to two, especially when one is so much greater than the other. One should also realise that the finger, the hand, or any limb loves the person it belongs to far more dearly than itself, and will willingly, happily and without question endure pain for that person. I declare with assurance and in truth that such a member cares absolutely nothing for itself except for the sake of that, and in that, of which it is a member. Accordingly it would only be right and proper, and in conformity with our nature, if we loved ourselves solely for God's sake and in God. And if that were so, then everything would be easy and pleasant for us that God wanted from us and in us, especially if we realised that God could much less tolerate any lack or loss, if He did not know and intend a much greater advantage from it. Indeed, if a man has no trust in God on that score, it is quite right that he should have pain and sorrow.

Here is another consolation. St Paul says that God chastens

all whom He accepts and receives as sons (cf. Heb. 12:6). Sonship involves suffering. Because God's Son could not suffer in the Godhead and in eternity, the heavenly Father sent him into time, to become man and suffer. So, if you want to be God's son and yet do not want to suffer, you are wrong. In the Book of Wisdom it says that God proves and tests to find out who is righteous, as we prove and test gold by fire in a furnace (Sap. 3:5–6). It is a sign that a king or a prince trusts a knight when he sends him into battle. I have seen one lord who sometimes, when he had taken a man into his retinue, would send him out by night and then attack him and fight with him. And once it happened that he was nearly killed by a man he wanted to test in this way; and he was much fonder of that retainer afterwards than before.

We read that St Antony was once especially sorely beset in the desert by evil spirits, and when he had transcended his suffering, our Lord appeared in visible form to him, rejoicing. Then the holy man said: 'Alas, dear Lord, where were you just now when I was in such great distress?' And our Lord said: 'I was here, just as I am now. I wanted to see, and was delighted to see how brave you were,'[53] A piece of silver or gold may well be pure, but if they want to make a cup for the king to drink out of it, they fire it much more thoroughly than another. Thus it says that the apostles rejoiced that they were worthy to endure contumely for God's sake (Acts 5:41). But God's Son by nature wished by his grace to become man so that he might suffer for you, and you want to become God's son and not man, so that you cannot and need not suffer for God's sake or your own! Also, if a man would only remember and consider what great joy God truly has in His own way, and all the angels and all who know and love God have, at the patience of a man when he suffers sorrow and loss for God's sake, then indeed a man should be truly comforted by that fact alone. For a man will give his goods and suffer great distress to give joy to a friend or to do him a kindness.

Again, one should reflect, if a man had a friend who was in sorrow, pain and distress on his account, surely it would be proper to be with him and comfort him with his presence and with such consolation as he could give. Therefore our Lord says in the Psalms that He is with him in his sorrow (Ps. 34:18 [AV]). From this text we can derive seven lessons and seven kinds of comfort.

In the first place, what St Augustine says, that patience in uffering for God's sake is better, more precious, higher and nobler than anything that a man can be deprived of against his will — which is nothing but outward goods.[54] God knows, you will find no man who loves this world, who is so rich that he would not gladly endure great pain, and put up with it for a long time, if thereafter he might be the paramount ruler of this world.

Secondly, I take it not only in the words that God utters, that He is with a man in his troubles, but I take it from, and in the text, and declare: if God is with me in my suffering, what more do I want, what else do I want? Surely I want nothing else, nothing more than God if I am in a right state? St Augustine says: 'Most greedy and unwise is he who is not satisfied with God',[55] and elsewhere he says: 'How should God's gifts to creatures satisfy a man who is not satisfied with God Himself?'[56] Therefore he says again elsewhere: 'Lord, if thou rejectest us, give us another thee, for we desire none but thee.'[57] Thus it says in the Book of Wisdom: "With God, the eternal Wisdom, all good things have come to me at once"

(Sap. 7:11). This means, in one sense, that nothing is or can be good that comes without God, and whatever comes with God is good, and is good only *because* it comes from God. Of God I will not speak. If we took from all creatures in the world the Being that God gives, they would remain as a mere nothing, unpleasing, valueless, hateful. This saying, that all goodness comes from God, has many other admirable meanings, too long to enter into here. Our Lord says: "I am with a man in his trouble" (Ps. 91:15 [AV]). Concerning this, St Bernard says: 'Lord, if thou art with us in suffering, let me suffer always, that thou mayest always be with me, so that I may always have thee.'[58]

Thirdly, I say that God's being with us in suffering means that He suffers with me Himself. Truly, he who knows the truth knows that I speak truth. God suffers with man, indeed, He suffers in His fashion before, and far more than that man who suffers for His sake. So I declare, if God Himself wills to suffer, then it is only right that I should suffer, for if it is well with me, then I want what God wants. I pray every day, and God bids me pray: "Lord, thy will be done",[59] and yet, when God wants suffering, I complain at the suffering, which is quite wrong. I also declare of a surety that God is so fond of suffering with us and for us if *we* suffer purely for God's sake, that He suffers without suffering. To suffer is such joy to Him that suffering for Him is no suffering.[60] And so, if we were in a right state, our suffering would be no suffering but a joy and a comfort.

Fourthly, I say that a friend's sympathy naturally eases my pain. So, if the suffering a human being shares with me brings comfort, how much more will God's sympathy[61] comfort me!

Fifthly, if I were ready and willing to suffer with a human being I was fond of and who was fond of me, then it is right that I should be willing to suffer with God, who suffers with me for the love He bears me.

Sixthly, I declare, if God suffers in advance, before I suffer, and if I suffer for God's sake, then indeed all my suffering, however great and manifold it may be, can easily turn to comfort and joy. It is a natural truth that if a man does something for another purpose, then that for which he does it is closer to his heart, and what he does is further from his heart and does not concern him except for the sake of that on account of which and for which it was done. If a builder hews wood and carves stone for the sole purpose of making a house against the heat of summer and the chill of winter, his heart is set first and solely on the house, and he would never hew the stone or endure the toil, but for the house. We observe that when a sick man drinks wine, he thinks and says it is bitter, and this is true, [62] for the wine loses all its sweetness through the external bitterness of the tongue, before it can get inside, where the soul can recognise and judge the flavour. So it is, and far more so, and more truly so, when a man does everything for God's sake, that God is the mediator and closest to the soul, and then nothing can touch a man's heart and soul without perforce losing its bitterness through God and God's sweetness, becoming pure sweetness before ever it can touch the man's heart.

Another testimony or comparison is this: the masters say that below heaven there is fire all round about, and therefore no wind or rain or storm or tempest can approach heaven from below near enough to touch it: it is all burnt up and destroyed by the heat of the fire before it gets near heaven. [63] Even so, I say that whatever one suffers or does for God's sake, that is all sweetened in God's sweetness before it reaches that man's heart who works and suffers for God's sake. For that is what is meant by the words 'for God's sake', because it never gets to the heart except by passing through God's sweetness in which it loses its bitterness. And it is burnt by the fiery flames of God's love, which envelops the good man's heart on all sides.

Now we can clearly perceive how well, and in how various ways, a good man is consoled on all sides in suffering, in sorrow, and in action. One way, if he suffers and works for God's sake, and another way, if he is in divine love. And a man can also tell and know if he is doing all his works for God's sake, and if he is in God's love; for assuredly, if a man finds himself woeful and disconsolate, to that extent his work was not done for God alone, and — observe! — to that extent he is not quite in God's love. King David says: "A fire comes with God and before God, that burns up all round about whatever God finds opposed to Him and unlike Him" (Ps. 97:3 [AV]), that is grief, disconsolateness, unrest and bitterness.

The seventh point about the saying that God is with us in suffering and suffers with us is: we should be profoundly comforted by the fact of Gd's being purely One without any adventitious quantity of difference even in thought, so that everything that is in Him is God Himself.[64] And since this is true, I say: whatever a good man suffers for God's sake, he suffers in God, and God is with him in his suffering. If my suffering is in God and God suffers with me, how then can my suffering be painful when suffering loses its pain, and my pain is in God and my pain *is* God?[65] In truth, as God is truth

95

and wherever I find truth I find my God, the truth — so likewise, neither more nor less, whenever I find pure suffering in God and for God, there I find God, my suffering. Whoever cannot understand this should blame his own blindness, not me or God's truth and loving-kindness.

Suffer therefore in this fashion for God's sake, since it brings such great profit and blessing. Our Lord says: "Blessed are they that suffer for righteousness' sake" (Matt. 5:10). How can God, who loves goodness, endure that his friends, good people, are not all the time suffering without a break? If a man had a friend who was to suffer a few days in order to gain great profit, honour and advantage, and possess that for a long time, then if he wanted to hinder this or if his wish were for someone to hinder it, people would not say he was that man's friend or fond of him. Therefore it may well be that God could in no way endure that His friends, good people, were ever without suffering, if they could not suffer without suffering. All the goodness of outward suffering comes forth and flows from the will, as I have written before. And therefore, whatever a good man would suffer, and is ready and eager to suffer for God's sake, that he *does* suffer before God's face, for God's sake in God. King David says in the Psalms: "I am ready in all distress, and my sorrow is ever present in my heart and in my face" (Ps. 38:18 [AV]). St Jerome says that a piece of wax that is soft and suitable to make out of it whatever one might wish, contains within itself all that can be made from it, even though outwardly no one should make anything out of it.[66] I too have written above that a stone is no less heavy when it is not lying visibly on the ground: all its heaviness is perfectly present in its tending downwards and being in itself ready to fall down. I have also written above that a good man has already done everything in heaven and earth that he wanted to do, in this respect just like God.

Now we can see the dullness of people who are commonly surprised when they see good people suffering pain and distress, and they often get the idea and the notion that this is due to their secret sins. And sometimes they say: 'Oh, I thought he was such a good man. How is it that he has to endure such great pain and sorrow? I thought he had no faults.' I agree that if it were really painful, and if they actually suffered in pain and distress, then they would not be good and sinless. But if they are good, then their suffering is no pain or misfortune, but a great happiness and blessing. "Blessed", said God, who is truth, "are they that suffer for righteousness' sake" (Matt. 5:10). And so the Book of Wisdom says that "The souls of the righteous are in God's hand. Foolish folk think and believe that they die and perish, but they are at peace" (Sap. 3:1—3). When St Paul describes how many saints have endured many sorts of pain, he says that the world was unworthy of them (Heb. 11:36—38), and this saying contains, rightly understood, three meanings. One is that the world is unworthy of the presence of many good people. Another sense is better, namely that the goodness of this world is despicable and worthless: God alone is of value, and therefore they are worthy in God's eyes and worthy of God. The third sense, that I mean now, and shall declare, is that this world, that is to say those that love this world, are unworthy to endure pain and distress for God's sake. Therefore it is written that the holy apostles rejoiced that they were worthy to endure pain in God's name (Acts 5:41).

Now enough of words, for in the third part of this book I want to describe many a comfort with which a good man should and may console himself in his sorrow, as can be found in the deeds, and not just in the words, of good and wise people.

III

We read in the Book of Kings that a man cursed King David and grossly insulted him. Then one of David's friends said he would slay the dirty dog. But the king said: "No! for it may be that God intends my welfare by this insult" (2 Kings [=2 Samuel AV] 16:5). In the *Book of the Fathers*[67] it says that a man lamented to a holy father that he was suffering. The father said: 'My son, do you want me to ask God to take this from you?' The other replied: 'No, father, for it is good for me — I know that well. But pray to God to give me His grace to bear it willingly.'

Once a sick man was asked why he did not pray to God to make him well. He said he was unwilling to do this for three reasons. One was that he felt sure a loving God would never tolerate his being sick unless it were for his good. The second was that if a man is good he wants whatever God wants, and not that God should want what man wants: that would not be right. And therefore, if He wants me to be ill — and if He did not, I should not be — then I ought not to wish to be well. For without doubt, if it were possible for God to make me well against His will, I would not want to care that He had made me well. Willing comes from loving, not-willing from not-loving. It is far preferable, better and more profitable for me that God loves me and I am sick, than if I were well in body and God did not love me. What God loves is something, and what God does not love is nothing, says the Book of Wisdom (cf. Sap. 11:25). And it is the truth that whatever God wills, precisely in and because of the fact that God wills it, is good. In truth, humanly speaking, I would rather that a rich and powerful man, a king, might love me and yet leave me for a while unrewarded, than that he should immediately bid them give me something without loving me — if he gave me nothing now out of love, postponing the gift because he intended to reward me better and more richly later on. Let us even suppose that the man who loves me and gives me nothing now has no intention of giving me anything; perhaps he will change his mind later and give me something. I must wait patiently, especially since his gift is by grace and is undeserved. But certainly, if I care nothing for a man's love and am opposed to his will, except that I want his gift, then it is right that he should give me nothing and should hate me and should leave me in misery.

The third reason why I scorn and dislike to ask God to make me well is that I will not and ought not to pray to the mighty, loving and generous God for such a small thing. Suppose I came to the Pope a hundred or two hundred miles, and when I came into his presence I were to say: 'My Lord, Holy Father, I have travelled about two hundred miles with great difficulty and expense, and I beg you — and this is what I came for — to give me a bean', truly, he and whoever heard it would say, and rightly, that I was a great fool. But it is a certain truth, I declare, that all goods, indeed all creatures, are less compared with God than a bean compared with the entire physical world. And so, if I were a good and wise man, I should rightly scorn to pray that I might be made well.

As regards this I say too that it is a sign of infirmity of mind if a man is joyful or sorrowful for the transient things of this world. We ought to be heartily ashamed before God and His angels and before men, if we notice such a thing in ourselves. [68] People are terribly ashamed of some defect in the face which shows *outwardly*. What more should I say? The books of the Old and New Testaments, the works of the saints and of the pagans are full of examples of how virtuous men have given up their lives and abandoned self for God's sake, or even from natural virtue.

A pagan master, Socrates, says that virtue makes impossible things possible, even easy and pleasant. [69] Nor would I forget that blessed lady of whom the Book of Maccabees tells, [70] who once saw before her eyes and heard the inhuman and grisly tortures inflicted on her seven sons; and she saw this joyfully and enjoined them all individually not to be afraid and to sacrifice body and soul willingly for the sake of God's justice.

Here we should end this book. But first, two more things.

One is this: certainly a good and godly man should be terribly ashamed at ever being moved by sorrow when we see that a merchant, for the sake of a small profit or even on a mere chance frequently goes on long journeys and perilous ways through mountains and valleys, wildernesses and seas, braving robbers and killers of his life and property, enduring great privations of food and drink, sleep, and other discomforts, and yet gladly and willingly forgets all this for such a small and doubtful gain. A knight in battle risks property, body and soul for fleeting and brief honour, and yet we think it so great a thing that we endure a little suffering for the sake of God and eternal blessedness.

The other thing I want to tell you is that many a dull-witted man will declare that a lot of the things I have said in this book and elsewhere are not true. To this I reply with what St Augustine says in the first book of his *Confessions*.[71] He says God has now made all future things for thousands and thousands of years (if the world should last so long), and that He will make today all things which have passed away many thousand years ago. How can I help it if anyone does not understand this? And elsewhere he says that that man is obviously too fond of himself who wants to blind others to hide his own blindness.[72] I am satisfied if what I say and write is true in me and in God. He who sees a stick[73] thrust into the water thinks the stick is crooked, although it is quite straight; this is due to the water being denser than the air. But the stick *is* straight, not crooked, both in itself and in the eyes of him who sees it in clear air.

St Augustine says: 'He who, free from all thoughts, all bodily forms and images, perceives within himself that which no outward seeing has conveyed to him, knows that this is true. But he who does not know this laughs and mocks at me, and I pity him. But such people want to behold and taste eternal things and divine activities, and stand in the light of eternity, while yet their heart is flitting about in yesterday and tomorrow.'[74]

A pagan master, Seneca, says: 'Great and lofty things should be discussed with great and lofty minds and with exalted souls.'[75] And some will say that such teachings should not be uttered or written to the unlearned. To this I reply: if one may not teach the unlearned, then no one can teach or write. For we teach the unlearned so that from being unlearned they may become learned. If there were nothing new there would be nothing old. "Those who are well", says our Lord, "have no need of medicine" (Luke 5:31). The physician is there to heal the sick. But if anyone misinterprets this saying, how can he help it who rightly teaches this saying, which is right? St John proclaims the holy gospel to all believers and also to all unbelievers that they may believe, and yet he begins his gospel with the highest that any man can declare here on earth about God; and *his* words, and those of our Lord, have frequently been misunderstood.

May the loving compassionate God, the Truth, grant to me and to all who read this book, that we may find truth within ourselves and become aware of it. Amen.

Notes

1. Cf. Vol. II, Appendix, and Nos 43 (II, p. 3) and 59 (II, pp. 97ff).
2. Cf. No. 80 (II, p. 236).
3. Cf. No. 21 (I, p. 175).
4. *Enarratio in Psalm* 36, 1,3 (PL 36, 357) (Q).
5. Cf. No. 59 (II, p. 98).
6. Cf. No. 65 (II, p. 133) and No. 66 (II, p. 146).
7. Cf. No. 68 (II, 161).
8. Cf. 1 Cor. 10:13.
9. Cf. Augustine, *Conf.* VII, ch. 12, n. 18; Aristotle, *Nic. Eth.* IV, ch. 12 (Q).
10. Cf. Augustine, *Conf.* X, ch. 41, n. 66 (Q).
11. Cf. Augustine, Sermon 105, n. 3,4 (PL 38, 620) (Q).
12. Not certainly traced.
13. Cf. No. 66 (II, p. 146).
14. Cf. Aristotle, *Physics* 4, ch. 1, 208a, 27ff. (Q). Cf. also No. 75 (II, p. 208).
15. Augustine, *De quantitate animae*, ch. 6, n. 9 (PL 32), 1040) (Q).
16. Seneca, *Nat. quaest.* III, praef. no. 12 (Q).
17. Also Seneca, *Epist. ad Lucilium* 107, 11, inaccurately quoted by Augustine in *De civ. Dei* V, ch. 8 (Q).
18. Cf. No. 57 (II, p. 84f.).
19. Condemned in article 14 of the Bull of 1329.
20. The value of what he has lost is 'credited' to him by God.

21. *De Trinitate* VIII, ch. 3, n. 4 (Q). The next passage, down to 'there and nowhere else', is not in Pfeiffer and therefore not translated by Miss Evans.

22. I.e. 'in truth'.

23. Cf. *Talks of Instruction*, § 7.

24. *Enarratio in Ps. 30*, sermo 3, n. 11 (Q).

25. Aristotle, *De anima* II, t.71 (Q). Cf. No. 19 (I, p. 160), No. 57 (II, p. 87), No. 69 (II, p. 168), No. 83 (II, p. 252).

26. Cf. No. 68 (II, p. 159f.).

27. Thomas, *Summa Theol*. I/II Q 3 A 2 ad 4, Q 3 A 4 and 5 (Q).

28. The first three of the seven gifts of the Holy Spirit (Gal. 5:22) (Clark). Cf. No. 87 (II, p. 273).

29. Cf. No. 4 (I, p. 44).

30. God the Father, the unbegotten begetter.

31. Cf. n. 14 above.

32. Cf. No. 45 (II, p. 16).

33. Cf. No. 59 (II, p. 98f.), where Eckhart quotes Is. 62:1.

34. Cf. No. 24a (I, p. 189).

35. Eckhart says 'you'.

36. Cf. No. 43 (II, p. 5).

37. Thomas, *Summa theol*. I, Q 13 A 7 ad 6 (Q).

38. Cf. No. 45 (II, p. 16) and LW III, 188, 13ff.

39. Cf. No. 32a (I, p. 238).

40. Cf. *Talks of Instruction*, 10, and No. 57 (II, p. 84f.).

41. Cf. No. 72 (II, p. 189).

42. Cf. e.g. No. 53 (II, p. 61).

43. Cf. No. 21 (I, p. 172).

44. Cf. Augustine, *De doctrina Christ*. III, ch. 27 n. 38 (Q).

45. This is the *Glossa ordinaria*, the famous Bible commentary by Walafrid Strabo of Reichenau (d. 849), widely used throughout the Middle Ages.

46. Cf. Peter Lombard, *Sentences* I, d. 9, c. 4 (Q).

47. Cf. Vol. I, Introduction, pp. xxxv–xxxvi.

48. Cf. No 62 (II, p. 114) and No. 24a (I, p. 188).

49. Cf. No. 7 (I, p. 67f.). Eckhart is punning on the two senses of the verb *ûfheben* 'take up', and 'take away, cancel'.

50. Cf. No. 40 (I, p. 283).

51. Eckhart's own expanded paraphrase of the scriptural text, summing up his interpretation just given.

52. Cf. No. 82 (II, p. 244).

53. *Lives of the Fathers* I, ch. 9 (PL 73, 132) (Q).

54. *Letters*, ch. 3, n. 12 (Q).

55. Cf. n. 10.

56. Cf. n. 11.

57. Cf. n. 12.

58. St Bernard, *In Psalmos* 90, sermo 7, n. 4 (Q).

59. Cf. No. 12 (I, p. 108) and No. 18 (I, p. 149).

60. Cf. St Augustine, *De Patientia* ch. 1, n. 1 (Clark).

61. Clark notes the play on the two meanings of *mitleiden*: 'suffering with another' and 'sympathy'. In fact the German word is a literal rendering of Latin *compassio* (= Greek *sympatheia*). This play on words is continued under the fifth head.

62. Cf. *Talks of Instruction* 11, and No. 53 (II, p. 65f.) and No. 68 (II, p. 161).

63. Cf. n. 14.

64. Cf. No. 25 (I, p. 199) and n. 5 there.

65. Conjectural restoration of a corrupt text by Quint. Clark says 'a bold and original thought' (i.e. that God *is* the mystic's suffering), but it is a typically Eckhartian deduction from the premise above (n. 64).

66. Cf. St Jerome, *Ep. CXX*, ch. 10 (PL 22, 999) (Q).

67. *Vitae Patrum* III (PL 73, 742, n. 8) (Q).

68. Clark renders: 'That one ever took any notice of them'. I follow Quint's interpretation: we should be ashamed, not at noticing 'things' but at the realisation that we are thus affected by them. This *outward* defect should be a greater cause of shame than any *inward* blemish. Miss Evans's rendering, 'We ought to be heartily ashamed to be found guilty of it . . .', is more of a paraphrase than a translation, but hits the meaning, assuming it is we who find *ourselves* 'guilty'.

69. Cf. *Platonis Timaeus interprete Chalcidio* (ed. J. Wrobel, Leipzig 1876), 210, 26ff. (Q).

70. 2 Maccabees, ch. 7.

71. *Confessions* I, ch. 6, n. 10 (Q). Clark by an oversight has 'the second book'.

72. Cf. *Confessions* X, ch. 23, n. 34 (Q).

73. Augustine actually says 'an oar': cf. *De Vera Religione* ch. 33, n. 62 (Q).

74. *Confessions* XI, ch. 8, n. 10 (Q).

75. *Epistolae* 71, 24 (Q).

III
THE NOBLEMAN

Our Lord says in the gospel: "A certain nobleman went away to a distant country to gain a kingdom for himself, and returned" (Luke 19:12). With these words our Lord teaches us how nobly man has been created by nature and how divine is that state to which he may attain by grace, and also how a man can come to this. And in these words a great part of holy scripture is touched upon.

One should first know, and it is in fact obvious, that man has two kinds of nature: body and spirit. Accordingly it says in one book: 'Whoever knows himself knows all creatures, for all creatures are either body or spirit'. [1] Thus too the scriptures say of man that there is in us an outer man and another, inner man. [2] To the outer man belongs all that is attached to the soul but embraced by and mixed with the flesh, and co-operating with and in each bodily member such as the eye, the ear, the tongue, the hand, and so on. And scripture calls all that the old man, the earthly man, the outward man, the hostile man, the servile man. [3] The other man who is within us is the inner man, whom scriptures call a new man, a heavenly man, a young man, a friend and a nobleman. And it is he whom our Lord means when he says: "A nobleman went away to a distant country, and gained a kingdom for himself, and returned."

It should also be known that St Jerome, and the masters in general, declare that every man, from the beginning of his human career, has a good spirit, an angel, and an evil spirit, a devil. [4] The good angel advises and continually inclines him to that which is good, that is godly, that is virtue and heavenly and eternal. The evil spirit advises and inclines the man continually to that which is temporal and transient, to what is sinful, evil and devilish. This same evil spirit for ever woos the outer man, and through him ever secretly plots against the inner man, just as the serpent wooed Lady Eve and, through her, the man Adam (Gen. 3:1–6). The inner man is Adam. The man in the soul[5] is the good tree that continually brings forth good fruits, of which our Lord speaks (Matt. 7:17). He is also the field in which God has sown His own image and likeness and in which He now sows the good seed (Matt. 13:24), the root of all wisdom, all arts, all virtues, all goodness, the seed of the divine nature. The seed of divine nature is God's Son, God's Word (Mark 4:3, Luke 8:11).

The outer man is the hostile man and the enemy who has sown and cast tares on the field (Matt. 13:25). Of him St Paul says: "I find within me that which hinders me and is opposed to what God commands and what God enjoins and what God has spoken and still speaks in the highest, in the ground of my soul" (cf. Rom. 7:23). And again he says and laments: "Oh wretched man that I am, who shall deliver me from this mortal flesh and body?" (Rom. 7:24). And elsewhere he says yet again that the spirit of man and his flesh are constantly fighting with each other (Gal. 5:17). The flesh counsels to vice and evil, the spirit counsels to the love of God, joy, peace and all virtues. Whoever follows and lives after the spirit, according to its counsel, belongs to eternal life.

The inner man is he of whom our Lord says: "A nobleman went away to a distant country to gain a kingdom for himself." That is the good tree of which our Lord says that it always brings forth good fruits and never evil (Matt. 7:18), for he wills the good and tends towards the good, and to goodness resting in itself and untouched by *this* and *that*. The outer man is the evil tree that can never bring forth good fruit.

Concerning the nobility of the inner man, of the spirit, and the worthlessness of the outer man, the flesh, the pagan masters Tully[6] and Seneca[7] also say that no rational soul is without God: God's seed is within us. If it had a good, skilful and industrious gardener to tend it, it would thrive all the better and grow up to God, whose seed it is, and the fruit would be like God's nature. The seed of a pear-tree grows into a pear-tree, that of a nut-tree into a nut-tree, God's seed into God. But if the good seed has a foolish or bad gardener, then weeds will grow and cover up and drive out the good seed so that it cannot reach the light and grow. But Origen, a great master, says: 'Since God Himself has sown this seed, impressed and impregnated it, it can indeed be covered over and hidden, but never destroyed or extinguished in itself; it glows and gleams, shines and burns and inclines without ceasing towards God.'[8]

The *first* stage of the inner man and the new man, St Augustine says, is that a man lives by the example of good and saintly people, though he still holds on to chairs and supports himself by walls, and subsists on milk.[9]

The *second* stage is when he not merely regards the outward examples and good people, but runs and hastens to the teaching and counsel of God and divine wisdom, turns his back on mankind and his face towards God, crawling forth from his mother's lap to smile up at his heavenly Father.

The *third* stage is when a man withdraws more and more

from his mother and, being further and further from her lap, escapes from care and casts off fear so that, even if he might with impunity do evil and injustice to all, he would have no wish to do so, for he is so bound to God with love in eagerness, until God establishes and leads him in joy, sweetness and bliss, wherein he cares nothing for whatever is repugnant and alien to God.

The *fourth* stage is when he grows more and more, and becomes rooted in love and in God, so that he is ready to welcome any trial, temptation, adversity and suffering willingly, gladly, eagerly and joyfully.

The *fifth* stage is when he lives altogether at peace with himself, resting calmly in the richness and abundance of the supreme ineffable wisdom.

The *sixth* stage is when a man is de-formed and trans-formed[10] by God's eternity, and has attained total forgetfulness of transitory, temporal life and is drawn and translated into a divine image, having become the child of God. Beyond this there is no higher stage,[11] and *there* there is eternal rest and bliss, for the final end of the inner man and the new man is eternal life.

Concerning this inner, noble man in whom God's seed and God's image are impressed and sown, and how the seed and the image of divine nature and divine being, God's Son, appears and is made manifest — but, too, is sometimes concealed — the great master Origen gives a simile:[12] that God's image, God's Son, is in the ground of the soul like a living fountain. If earth is thrown on it (that is, earthly desire), that hinders and covers it up so that it is not recognised or perceived; yet it remains living within, and when the earth that was thrown on to it from without is removed, it appears visibly. He says this truth is indicated in the First Book of Moses, where it says that Abraham had dug wells of living water in his field, and evil-doers filled them with earth, and later when the earth was removed the living streams reappeared (cf. Gen. 26:15ff.).

Here is another simile: the sun is always shining but, if there is a cloud or fog between us and the sun, we do not perceive its radiance. Likewise, if the eye is weak and sick in itself, or is covered over, it perceives no light. I have also sometimes used a clear example: if an artist wants to make an image from wood or stone, he does not put the image into the wood, but he cuts away the chips that had hidden and concealed the image: he *gives* nothing to the wood but *takes* from it, cutting away the overlay and removing the dross, and then that which was hidden under it shines forth. That is the treasure hidden in a field of which our Lord tells in the gospel (Matt. 13:44).

St Augustine says that when the soul is turned entirely upward into eternity, into God alone, then God's image shines forth and glows; but when the soul is turned outwards, if only to the outward practice of virtue, then the image is totally veiled. [13] And that is why women's heads are covered and men's bare, according to St Paul's teaching (1 Cor. 11:4–5). [14] Thus, whatever of the soul turns downwards receives a covering, a kerchief, from what it turns to; but that in the soul which turns upwards, *that* is God's bare image, God's birth, bare and naked in the naked soul. [15] In the noble man, just as in God's image, God's son, the seed of divine nature can never be destroyed in us though it may be covered up. King David says in the Psalms: "Although man is afflicted by many kinds of vanity, suffering and distress, he shall abide in God's image and the image in him."[16] The true light shines in the darkness though we may be unaware of it (cf. John 1:5).

"Do not consider", says the Book of Love, "that I am brown, for I am shapely and beautiful, only the sun has discoloured me a little" (Cant. 1:5).[17] The sun is the light of this world, and this means that the highest and best of things created or made will hide and discolour the image of God within us. "Take away", says Solomon, "the dross from the silver, and the purest of vessels will gleam and shine forth" (Prov. 25:4),[18] that is the image, God's son, in the soul. And that is what our Lord meant by these words, that "a nobleman went forth", for a man must go out from all forms and from himself, become wholly foreign and remote from them all, if he really means to receive the Son and become the Son in God's bosom and heart.

All that is a 'means' is alien to God. God says: "I am the first and the last" (Is. 41:4; Rev. 22:13). There is no distinction either in God's nature, or in the Persons according to the unity of that nature. The divine nature is One, and each Person is also one and is the same One that the nature is.[19] The distinction of being and essence is taken as one and is one. Where it is not present, it assumes, has and creates distinction. And so: in the One, God is found, and he who would find God must become one. "A man", our Lord says, "went out". In distinction one can find neither being, nor God, nor rest, nor bliss, nor satisfaction. Be one, that you may find God! And in truth, if you were truly one, then you would even remain one in difference, and difference would be one to you, and then nothing could hinder you. One remains equally one in a thousand times a thousand stones as in four as in four stones, and a thousand times a thousand is just a simple number as four is a number.

A pagan master says that One is born of the supreme God.[20] Its property is being one with one. Whoever seeks it beneath God, deceives himself. And in the fourth place the same master says that this One has real friendship with none so much as with virgins or maidens, as St Paul says: "I have espoused and promised you chaste virgins to the One" (2 Cor. 11:2). And that is how a man should be, for so says our Lord: "One man went out".

'Man' in the proper meaning of his name in Latin[21] means in one sense one who bows and submits himself wholly to God, all that he is and all that is his, looking upward to God, and not his possessions which he knows to be behind him, below him and beside him. This is perfect and genuine humility: the name comes from the earth (*humus*). I shall say no more of this for now. Further, when we say 'man', the word means something that is above nature, above time and above whatever inclines to time or smacks of time, and I say the same too of place and corporeality. Furthermore, this man has in one sense nothing in common with anything, that is, he is not formed or likened to *this* or *that*, and knows nothing of 'nothing', so that one only finds in him pure life, being, truth and goodness. A man of this sort is a 'noble man' indeed, neither more nor less.

There is still another way of explaining what our Lord terms a noble man. You should know that those who know God naked, also know creatures with Him: for knowledge is a light of the soul, all men desire knowledge,[22] for even the knowledge of evil things is good.[23] The masters say that when one knows creatures in themselves, that is evening knowledge,[24] for then one sees the creatures in images of varied distinction; but when one sees creatures in God, that is called morning knowledge, and then one sees creatures without all distinction, stripped of form and deprived of all 'likeness',[25] in the One that is God Himself. This too is the noble man of whom our Lord said: "A nobleman went out" — noble because he is one and because he knows God and creatures in the One.

I would now refer to and discuss yet another sense of 'nobleman'. I say that when a man, the soul, the spirit, sees God, he realises and knows himself as knowing. That is, he knows that he sees and knows God. Now some people have thought, and it seems credible, that the flower and kernel of bliss lies in that knowledge, when the spirit knows that it knows God;[26] for if I had all joy and did not know it, what good would that be to me, and what joy would that be? But I definitely deny that that is so. Though it is true that the soul cannot be happy *without* that, yet felicity does not depend on it; for the *first* condition of felicity is that the soul sees God naked. From that she derives all her being and her life, and draws all that she is, from the ground of God, knowing nothing of knowledge, nor of love, nor of anything at all. She is utterly calm in God's being, knowing nothing but being there and God. But when she is aware and *knows* that she sees, knows and loves God, that is a turning away and a reversion to the former stage according to the natural order:[27] for none knows himself to be white but he who is white.[28] Therefore, he who knows himself to be white builds and supports himself on being-white: he does not receive his knowing without mediation or unknowingly, direct from the colour: he gets his knowledge of it and about it from that which is now white, not drawing knowledge and awareness from the colour alone and in itself; he gets knowledge and awareness from what is coloured or white, thus knowing himself to be white. White is much less, and much more external than whiteness. There is a big difference between the wall and the foundation on which the wall is built.

The masters say there is one power whereby the eye sees, and another by which it knows that it sees.[29] The first, *that* it sees, it gets from the colour, not from that which is coloured. Therefore it is all the same whether the coloured object is a stone or a block of wood, a man or an angel: all its essence lies in the fact that it has colour. So I say that the noble man receives and draws all his being, life and bliss from God, by God and in God alone and bare, and not from knowing, seeing or loving God or anything like that. Therefore our Lord says in very truth that eternal life is knowing God alone as true God, and not in knowing that one knows God (John 17:3).[30] How could a man know that he knows God, if he does not know himself? For indeed a man knows himself and other things not at all, but only God, when he gains felicity, in the root and ground of blessedness. But when the soul knows that she knows God, then she has knowledge of both God and herself.

Now there is one power, as I have said, whereby man sees, and another whereby he is aware and knows that he sees. It is true that here and now that power in us by which we are aware and know that we see is nobler and higher than the power by which we see; for nature begins her work at the weakest point, but God begins His work with the most perfect. Nature makes a man out of a child, and a hen out of an egg, but God makes the man before the child and the hen before the egg. Nature first makes wood warm and hot, and thereafter creates the essence of fire; but God *first* gives all creatures their being, and after that, in time yet timelessly,[31] He gives individually all that belongs to it [= to being]. And God gives the Holy Ghost before He gives the gifts of the Holy Ghost.

Therefore I say that there is no blessedness without a man's being aware and well knowing that he knows God — and yet, God forbid that my felicity should depend on that! If anyone is satisfied with that, let him have it, but I am sorry for him. The heat of the fire and the essence of fire are quite unlike and strangely remote from each other in nature, although very close in time and space.[32] God's seeing and our seeing are very distant and different from each other.

Therefore it was very well said by our Lord that "a nobleman went away to a distant country to gain a kingdom for himself, and returned". For man must be one in himself and must seek it in himself and in one — that is, to see God alone; and 'returning' is being aware and knowing that one knows God and is aware of it. And all this has been said before by the prophet Ezekiel, when he said that a mighty eagle with great wings, with long pinions, full of varied plumage, came to the pure mountain and, taking away the pith and marrow of the highest tree, cropped off its crown of leaves and brought it down (Ezek. 17:3). What our Lord calls a nobleman, the prophet calls a mighty eagle. Who then is nobler than he who is born, on the one hand from the highest and best that creatures have, and on the other hand from the innermost ground of divine nature and of His wilderness? In the prophet Hosea, our Lord says: "I will lead the noble soul into a wilderness, and there I will speak into her heart" (Hos.

2:14), one with One, one from One, one in One, and a single One eternally. Amen.

Notes

1. Isaac Israeli (d. 933), *Liber de Diffinitionibus* (Q).
2. Cf. 2 Cor. 4:16. Cf. No. 70 (II, p. 173).
3. For these cf. 1 Cor. 15:47; Matt. 13:28; Luke 19:13–15; Rom. 6:17.
4. Cf. St Jerome, *Comm. in Ev. Matt.* III, ch. 18, 10–11; Peter Lombard, *Sententiae* II, dist. 11, ch. 1, n. 74 (Q).
5. Cf. No. 36 (I, p. 265).
6. (M. Tullius) Cicero, *De Tusc. Quaest.* III, ch. 1, n. 2 (Q).
7. *Epist.* 73, 16 (Q).
8. *Homiliae in Genesim* 13, n. 4 (Q after Koch). Cf. also the refs. to *Synteresis* (I, Note A, p. xli) and No. 32a (I, p. 238). The orthodox view is that this spark is never extinguished even in the eternally damned. Origen did not believe in eternal damnation: 'To safeguard the liberty of rational souls, Origen thinks it necessary to regard them as ever capable of renewal; the sensible world, created by God for the purification of fallen souls, will come to an end when all will have been restored to their original purity' [*De principiis* III, vi, 6]: thus Origen's view is quoted with disapproval by Lebreton and Zeiller, *History of the Primitive Church* IV, transl. E. C. Messenger, London, 1948, 784f. This view was, alas, not accepted by the Church which saddled itself with the awful doctrine of eternal damnation, not least through the insistence of the otherwise reasonable Augustine. If Eckhart had any doubts about this doctrine, he perforce kept silent, but his reference to Origen here may be significant, and it is a fact that his references to hell are few and perfunctory (cf. Clark, *Meister Eckhart*, London 1957, p. 53). See also No. 57 (II, p. 85 and n. 5 there).
9. *De Vera Rel.* ch. 26, n. 9 (Q).
10. *entbildet und überbildet*: cf. No. 47 (II, p. 28 and n. 3 there).
11. Augustine has in fact a seventh stage.
12. Cf. n. 8 above.
13. *De Trin.* XII, ch. 7, n. 10 (Q).
14. Cf. No. 68 (II, p. 160).
15. Cf. No. 32a (I, p. 239).
16. Q says: 'Cf. Ps. 4:2ff.', and Blakney says: 'Possibly Psalm 17:9–15', while Clark declares: 'There is no such passage in the Psalter'. Certainly the parallels adduced are not close. Eckhart is quoting scripture very freely again to suit his

purpose — something which was never held against him!

17. Cf. No. 21 (I, p. 173). 18. Cf. No. 14b (I, p. 123f.).

19. Condemned in the Bull of 1329, art. 24. Cf. No. 66 (II, p. 145).

20. Macrobius, *In Somnium Scipionis* I, ch. 6, n. 7—10 (Q).

21. Cf. No. 20 (I, p. 166f.).

22. Aristotle, *Metaphysics* 1,1 (Q). Cf. No. 66 (II, p. 141).

23. Thomas, *Summa contra Gent.* I, 71 (Q). Cf. No. 82 (II, p. 247 and n. 19 there).

24. Augustine, *De Gen. ad Litt.* IV, ch. 23, n. 40 (Q). Cf. No. 82 (II, p. 245).

25. Lit. 'unlikened of all likeness' (*aller glîcheit entglîchet*).

26. Thomas, *Summa Theol.* II/I, Q 3. Cf. LW III, 93, 6ff.

27. All this paragraph is loosely quoted by Suso in his *Little Book of Eternal Wisdom* (transl. Clark, London 1953, p. 195).

28. As Clark notes, some MSS have *wîse* 'wise' for *wîz* 'white'. But there is no doubt as to the correct reading: as Quint points out, Eckhart several times refers in his Latin writings to the relation between 'whiteness' and 'white'.

29. More accurately stated at the beginning of the next paragraph, since it is the *man*, not his *eye*, that 'knows'. Cf. Thomas, *Summa Theol.* I, Q 78 A 4 ad 2 (Q).

30. The qualification is, of course, Eckhart's addition.

31. 'God gives the creatures existence, first in His mind as prototypes or ideas, and then as created beings in the visible universe' (Clark).

32. Cf. No. 95 (II, p. 326).

IV

ON DETACHMENT

I have read many writings of pagan masters, and of the prophets, and of the Old and New Testaments, and have sought earnestly and with all diligence to discover which is the best and highest virtue whereby a man may chiefly and most firmly join himself to God, and whereby a man may become by grace what God is by nature, and whereby a man may come closest to his image when he was in God,[1] wherein there was no difference between him and God, before God made creatures. After a thorough study of these writings I find, as well as my reason can testify or perceive, that only pure detachment surpasses all things, for all virtues have some regard to creatures, but detachment is free of all creatures. Therefore our Lord said to Martha: *"unum est necessarium"* (Luke 10:42), which is as much as to say, 'Martha, he who would be serene and pure needs but one thing: detachment'.

The teachers greatly praise love, as does St Paul who says: "Whatever things I may do, and have not love, I am nothing" (cf. 1 Cor. 13:1). But I extol detachment above any love. First, because, at best, love constrains me to love God, but detachment compels God to love me. Now it is a far nobler thing my constraining God to me than for me to constrain myself to God. That is because God is more readily able to adapt Himself to me, and can more easily unite with me than I could unite with God. That detachment forces God to me, I can prove thus: everything wants to be in its natural place. Now God's natural place is unity and purity, and that comes

117

from detachment. Therefore God is bound to give Himself to a detached heart.[2]

In the second place I extol detachment above love because love compels me to suffer all things for God's sake, whereas detachment makes me receptive of nothing but God. Now it is far nobler to be receptive of nothing but God than to suffer all things *for* God, for in suffering a man has some regard to the creatures from which he gets the suffering, but detachment is quite free of all creatures. But that detachment is receptive of nothing but God, I can prove this way: whatever is to be received must be taken in somewhere. Now detachment is so nearly nothing that there is no thing subtle enough to maintain itself in detachment except God alone. He is so subtle and so simple that He can stay in a detached heart. Therefore detachment is receptive of nothing but God.

The masters also extol humility above many other virtues. But I extol detachment above humility for this reason: humility can exist without detachment, but perfect detachment cannot exist without perfect humility, for perfect humility ends in the destruction of self. Now detachment comes so close to nothing, that between perfect detachment and nothing no thing can exist. Therefore perfect detachment cannot be without humility. But two virtues are always better than one.

The second reason why I praise detachment above humility is because humility means abasing onself beneath all creatures, and in that abasement man goes out of himself into creatures, but detachment rests within itself. Now no going out can ever be so noble, but remaining within is nobler still. As the prophet David says: "*Omnis gloria eius filiae regis ab intus*" (Ps. 45:13 [AV]), which is to say: "All the glory of the daughter comes from her inwardness". Perfect detachment is not concerned about being above or below any creature; it does not wish to be below or above, it would stand on its own, loving none and hating none, and seeks neither equality nor inequality with any creature, nor this nor that: it wants merely to be.[3] But to be either this or that it does not wish at all. For whoever would be this or that wants to be *something*, but detachment wants to be nothing. It is therefore no burden on anything.

Now somebody might say, 'Well, our Lady possessed all virtues to perfection, and so she must have had perfect detachment. But if detachment is higher than humility, why then did our Lady glory in her humility and not in her detachment when she said: "*Quia respexit dominus humilitatem ancillae suae*" (Luke 1:48), that is to say: "He regarded the humility of his handmaiden"?'

I reply that in God there is detachment *and* humility, in so far as we can speak of God's having virtues. You should know that it was loving humility that led God to stoop to enter human nature, while detachment stood immovable within itself when he became man, just as it did when He created heaven and earth, as I shall tell you later. And because our Lord, when he would become man, stood unmoved in his detachment, our Lady knew that he required the same of her too, and that in this case he looked to her humility and not her detachment. For if she had thought once about her detachment and said, 'he regarded my detachment', that detachment would have been sullied and would not have been whole and perfect, since a going forth would have occurred. But nothing, however little, may proceed from detachment without staining it. There you have the reason why our Lady

119

gloried in her humility and not her detachment. Concerning this, the prophet said: "*Audiam, quid loquatur in me dominus deus*" (Ps. 85:8 [AV]), that is to say: "I will (be silent and) hear what my lord God says within me", as if he were to say, 'If God wishes to speak to me, let Him come into me, for I will not go out.'

I also praise detachment above all compassion, for compassion is nothing but a man's going out of himself by reason of his fellow creatures' lack, by which his heart is troubled. But detachment is free of this, stays in itself and is not troubled by any thing: for as long as any thing can trouble a man, he is not in a right state. In short, when I consider all the virtues, I find none so completely without lack and so conformed to God as detachment.

A master called Avicenna[4] declares that the mind of him who stands detached is of such nobility that whatever he sees is true, and whatever he desires he obtains, and whatever he commands must be obeyed. And this you must know for sure: when the free mind is quite detached, it constrains God to itself, and if it were able to stand formless and free of all accidentals, it would assume God's proper nature. But God can give *that* to none but Himself, therefore God can do no more for the detached mind than give Himself to it. But the man who stands thus in utter detachmemt is rapt into eternity in such a way that nothing transient can move him, and that he is aware of nothing corporeal and is said to be dead to the world, for he has no taste for anything earthly. That is what St Paul meant when he said: "I live and yet do not live — Christ lives in me" (Gal. 2:20).

Now you may ask what this detachment is that is so noble in itself. You should know that true detachment is nothing else but a mind that stands unmoved by all accidents of joy or sorrow, honour, shame or disgrace, as a mountain of lead stands unmoved by a breath of wind. This immovable detachment brings a man into the greatest likeness to God. For the reason why God is God is because of His immovable detachment, and from this detachment He has His purity, His simplicity and His immutability. Therefore, if a man is to be like God, as far as a creature *can* have likeness with God, this must come from detachment. This draws a man into purity, and from purity into simplicity, and from simplicity into immutability, and these things make a likeness between God and that man; and this likeness must occur through grace, for grace draws a man away from all temporal things and purges him of all that is transient. You must know, too, that to be empty of all creatures is to be full of God, and to be full of all creatures is to be empty of God.

You should also know that God has stood in this unmoved detachment from all eternity, and still so stands; and you should know further that when God created heaven and earth and all creatures, this affected His unmoved detachment just as little as if no creature had ever been created. I say further: all the prayers and good works that a man can do in time affect God's detachment as little as if no prayers or good works had ever occurred in time, and God never became more ready to give or more inclined towards a man than if he had never uttered the prayer or performed the good works. I say still further: when the Son in the Godhead wanted to become man, and became man and endured martyrdom, *that* affected God's unmoved detachment as little as if he had never become man. You might say at this: 'Then I hear that all prayers and good works are wasted because God does not allow Himself to be moved by anyone with such things, and yet it is said that God wants us to pray to Him for everything.'

Now you should mark me well, and understand properly if you can, that God in His first eternal glance (if we can assume that there *was* a first glance) saw all things as they should occur, and saw in the same glance when and how He would create all creatures and when the Son would become man and suffer; He saw too the least prayer and good work that anyone should do, and saw which prayers and devotion He would and should accede to; He saw that you will call upon Him earnestly tomorrow and pray to Him, but God will not grant your petition and prayer tomorrow, for He *has* granted it in His eternity, before ever you became a man. But if your prayer is not sincere and in earnest, God will not deny it to you now, for He *has* denied it to you in His eternity.

And thus God has regarded all things in His first eternal glance, and God performs nothing afresh, for all has been performed in advance. Thus God ever stands in His immovable detachment, and yet the prayers and good works of people are not wasted, for he who does well will be rewarded, and he who does evil will reap accordingly. This is explained by St Augustine in the fifth book of *On the Trinity*, in the last chapter thus: *'Deus autem, &c.'*, which means: 'God forbid that anyone should say that God loves anyone in time, for with Him there is no past and no future, and He loved all the saints before the world was ever created, as He foresaw them. And when it comes to be that He displays in time what He has seen in eternity, then people think He has gained a new love for them; so too, when God is angry or does some good thing, it is we who are changed while He remains unchanged, just as the sun's ray hurts a sick eye and delights a sound one, and yet the sunshine remains unchanged in itself.' Augustine also touches on the same idea in the twelfth book of *On the Trinity* in the fourth chapter, where he says: '*Nam Deus non ad tempus videt, nec aliquid fit novi in eius visione*', 'God does not see in temporal fashion, and no new vision arises in Him.' In the same sense Isidore speaks in his book *On the Highest Good*,[5] saying: 'Many people ask: What did God do before He created heaven and earth, or whence came the new will in God that He made creatures?', and he answers: 'No new will ever arose in God, for although a creature did not exist in itself (as it is now), yet it was before all time in God and in His reason.'[6] God did not create heaven and earth as we (perishable beings) might say, 'let that be so!', for all creatures were spoken in the Eternal Word. To this we can add what our Lord said to Moses when Moses said: "Lord, if Pharaoh asks me who you are, how am I to answer him?", and the Lord said: "Say, 'He who IS has sent me'" (Ex. 3:13–14). That is as much as to say: 'He who is immutable in Himself has sent me.'

But someone might say, 'Was Christ in unmoved detachment when he said: "My soul is sorrowful even unto death" (Matt. 26:38; Mark 14:34), and Mary when she stood before the cross? How is all this compatible with unmoved detachment?' Concerning this, you should know what the masters say, that in every man there are two kinds of man.[7] The one is called the outer man, that is, the life of the senses: this man is served by the five senses, though the outer man functions by the power of the soul. The other is called the inner man, that is, man's inward nature. You should understand that a spiritual man, who loves God, makes use of the powers of the soul in the outer man only to the extent that the five outer senses need it: the inward nature is not concerned with the five senses except in so far as it is a guide or ruler of those senses, guarding them so that they do not yield to sense-objects in a bestial fashion, as some folk do who live for carnal pleasures like beasts unendowed with reason; such people should be termed beasts rather than men. And whatever powers the soul has over and above what it gives to the five senses are all devoted to the inner man. And when such a man perceives a noble or elevated object, the soul draws into itself all the powers it has granted to the five senses, and then that man is said to be insensible or entranced,[8] for his object is an intelligible image or something intelligible without an image.[9] But you should know that God requires of every spiritual man to love Him with all the powers of the soul. He says: "Love your God with all your heart" (Deut. 6:5; Matt. 22:37; Mark 12:30; Luke 10:27). Now some people use up all the powers of the soul in the outer man. These are people who turn all their senses and their reason towards perishable goods, knowing nothing of the inner man.

You should know that the outer man can be active while the inner man is completely free of this activity and unmoved. Now Christ too had an outer man and an inner man, and so did our Lady, and whatever Christ and our Lady ever said about external things, they did so according to the outer man, but the inner man remained in unmoved detachment. Thus it was when Christ said: "My soul is sorrowful unto death", and whatever lamentations our Lady made, or whatever else she said, inwardly she was in a state of unmoved detachment. Here is an analogy: a door swings open and shuts on its hinge. I would compare the outer woodwork of the door to the outer man, and the hinge to the inner man. When the door opens and shuts, the boards move back and forth, but the hinge stays in the same place and is never moved thereby. It is the same in this case, if you understand it rightly.

Now I ask: 'What is the object of pure detachment?' My answer is that the object of pure detachment is neither *this* nor *that*. It rests on absolutely nothing, and I will tell you why: pure detachment rests on the highest, and he is at his highest, in whom God can work all His will. But God cannot work all His will in all hearts, for, although God is almighty, He can only work where He finds readiness or creates it. I say 'creates it' on account of St Paul, because in him God found no readiness, but made him ready by infusion of grace. And so I say God works according as He finds us ready. His working is different in a man and in a stone. Here is an example from nature. If you heat a baker's oven and put in it dough of oats, barley, rye and wheat, there is only one heat in the oven, but it does not have the same effect on the different kinds of dough, for one turns into fine bread, the second coarser, and the third coarser still. And that is not the fault of the heat, it is due to the materials which are unlike. In the same way God does not work alike in all our hearts: He works as He finds readiness and receptivity. Now in whatever heart there is *this* or *that*, there may be something in 'this' or 'that' which God cannot bring to the highest peak. And so, if the heart is to be ready to receive the highest, it must rest on absolutely nothing, and in that lies the greatest potentiality which can exist. For when the detached heart rests on the highest, that can only be on nothing, since that has the greatest receptivity. Let us take an example from nature: if I want to write on a wax tablet, then anything written on that tablet already, however wonderful it may be, will prevent me from writing there; and if I want to write I must erase or destroy whatever is on the tablet, and the tablet is never so suitable for me to write on as when there is nothing on it. Similarly, if God is to write the highest on my heart, then everything called 'this and that' must be expunged from my heart, and then my heart stands in detachment. *Then* God can work the highest according to His supreme will. Therefore the object of a detached heart is neither this nor that.

Again I ask: 'What is the prayer of a detached heart?' My answer is that detachment and purity cannot pray, for whoever prays wants God to grant him something, or else wants God to take something from him. But a detached heart desires nothing at all, nor has it anything it wants to get rid of. Therefore it is free of all prayers, or its prayer consists of nothing but being uniform with God. That is all its prayer. In this sense we can take St Dionysius's comment on the saying of St Paul: "There are many who run, but only one gains the crown" (1 Cor. 9:25). All the powers of the soul compete for the crown but the essence alone can win it. Dionysius says the race is nothing but a turning away from all creatures and a union with the uncreated.[10] And when the soul has got so far, it loses its name and is drawn into God, so that in itself it becomes nothing, just as the sun draws the dawn into itself and annihilates it. To this state nothing brings a man but pure detachment. To this we may add a saying of St Augustine: 'The soul has a secret entrance to the divine nature, when all things become nothing for it.'[11] On earth, this entrance is nothing but pure detachment, and when the detachment reaches its climax, it becomes ignorant with knowing, loveless with loving, and dark with enlightenment. Thus we may understand the words of a master, that the poor in spirit are they who have abandoned all things to God, just as He possessed them when we did not exist.[12] None can do this but a pure, detached heart.

That God would rather be in a detached heart than in all other hearts, appears if you ask me: 'What does God seek in all things?', to which I answer from the Book of Wisdom, where He says: "In all things I seek rest" (Eccl. 24:11).[13] But nowhere is perfect rest to be found but in a detached heart. That is why God prefers to be there rather than in other virtues or in anything else. You should know, too, that the more a man strives to be receptive to divine influence, the more blessed he is; and whoever can gain the highest readiness in this is in the highest state of blessedness. But none can make himself receptive to divine influence but by uniformity with God, for in so far as a man is uniform with God, to that extent he is receptive to the divine influence. But uniformity comes from man's subjecting himself to God, and the more a man is subject to creatures, the less he is uniform with God. Now the pure detached heart stands free of all creatures. Therefore it is totally subject to God, and therefore it is in the highest degree of uniformity with God, and is also the most receptive to divine influence. This was what St Paul meant when he said: "Put on Christ,"[14] meaning unformity with Christ, for this putting on can only take place through uniformity with Christ. You should know that when Christ became man, he took on, not a man, but human nature.[15] Therefore, go out of all things and *then* there will remain only what Christ took on, and thus you will have put on Christ.

Whoever would know the nobility and profit of perfect detachment, let him note Christ's saying concerning his humanity, when he said to his disciples: "It is expedient for you that I should go away from you, for if I do not go away, the Holy Spirit cannot come to you" (John 16:7). [16] This is just as if he had said: 'You rejoice too much in my present form, and therefore the perfect joy of the Holy Ghost cannot be yours.' So, leave all images and unite with the formless essence, for God's spiritual comfort is delicate, therefore He will not offer Himself to any but to him who scorns physical comforts.

Now take note, all who are sensible! No man is happier than he who has the greatest detachment. There can be no fleshly and physical comfort without some spiritual harm, for "the flesh lusts against the spirit and the spirit against the flesh" (cf. Gal. 5:17). Therefore, whoever in the flesh sows disorderly love reaps death, and whoever in the spirit sows ordered love, reaps from the spirit eternal life. Therefore, the quicker a man flees from the created, the quicker the Creator runs towards him. So, take note, all sensible men! Since the joy we might have from the physical form of Christ hinders us in receiving the Holy Ghost, how much more of a hindrance to gaining God is our inordinate delight in evanescent comforts! That is why detachment is best, for it purifies the soul, purges the conscience, kindles the heart, awakens the spirit, quickens the desire, makes us know God and, cutting off creatures, unites us with God.

Now take note, all who have good sense! The swiftest steed to bear you to His perfection is suffering, for none will enjoy greater eternal bliss than those who stand with Christ in the greatest bitterness. Nothing is more gall-bitter than suffering, nothing more honey-sweet than having suffered. Nothing disfigures the body before men like suffering, and nothing beautifies the soul before God like having suffered. The finest foundation on which this perfection can rest is humility. For whatever man's nature creeps here below in the deepest lowliness, that man's spirit will soar aloft to the heights of the Godhead, for joy brings sorrow and sorrow joy. And so, whoever would attain perfect detachment should strive for perfect humility, and thus he will come to the neighbourhood of God. That this may be all our lot, so help us the highest detachment, which is God Himself. Amen.

Notes

1. As an idea in the mind of God. Cf. No. 58 (II, p. 90) and No. 87 (II, p. 271 and n. 7 there).

2. Cf. No. 73 (II, p. 197).

3. The variant reading *eine sîn* 'to be alone' is rejected by Quint, following Schaefer.

4. *Liber VI, Nat.*, pars 4, c. 4 (ed. of 1508) (Q). Skinner/Clark's ref. is wrong.

5. *Sent.* I, ch. 8, n. 4 (Q).

6. Cf. n. 1 above.

7. Cf. No. 56 (II, p. 80).

8. Not 'senseless or crazy' (Clark).

9. Quint cites Thomas, *De Veritate* Q 13 A 2 on the different degrees of absorption. These are reminiscent of the 'world of form' (*rūpaloka*) and the 'formless world' (*arūpaloka*) of Buddhism, which are attained by the practice of the *jhānas* ('absorptions').

10. *De divinis nom.* ch. 4, 9 and ch. 13, 3 (Quint after Fischer).

11. Not traced directly in Augustine's works.

12. Cf. No. 87 (II, p. 270f.).

13. Not the Wisdom of Solomon but Ecclesiasticus (The Wisdom of Jesus Sirach), as in No. 73 (II, p. 197); cf. No. 45 (II, p. 13).

14. Cf. No. 92 (II, p. 311 and n. 1 there).

15. Cf. No. 47 (II, p. 27 and n. 2 there).

16. Cf. No. 75 (II, p. 207).

V

FRAGMENT OF AN UNKNOWN
SERMON (98)[1]

. . . This word [i.e. 'widow'] means 'she who has been abandoned'.[2] It denotes a soul that is abandoned and *has* abandoned all creatures, as I have said before. There is a light in the soul where time and place have never entered. Whatever has ever touched time and place never came into this light. In this light a man should stand.[3] Our Lord said in a different place (Matt. 13:24f.) that a man sowed his seed in the field. While the people were sleeping, the enemy came and cast his evil seed therein. God has cast His seed in the soul.[4] His seed is His Word, His Son. He has given him into the midst of the soul. A man should rather give up and lose body and soul than lose God.[5] The heart lies in the middle of the body. The masters say that God and nature have set the heart in the middle of the body so that a man may abandon all his members to death and destruction rather than lose his heart.[6] God has put His seed, His Word, in the middle of the soul, so that a man may lose all that he can achieve rather than lose God.[7] When God creates the soul, He begets His only-begotten Son in her, and perhaps before. I say, when God creates the soul, He creates the soul and begets His only-begotten Son into the soul both at once in one moment, at the same time and above time:[8] thus He pours His image into the soul.[9] Our Lord says: "He cast his seed in the field. While the people were sleeping the enemy came and cast his evil seed among the wheat." When a man is not willing to guard himself against the world and against people from whom harm may come. . . .[10] Secondly, when the soul[11] . . . stands in the light and in the intellect[12] and in the highest light, then it is day in the soul[13] where God wants to sow His seed. The masters say the birth that occurs during the day is nobler than in the night on account of certain things that accompany it.[14] The people who are born by day are nobler than those born by night on account of certain things. Therefore he[15] says that the son of the barren woman is far nobler than the son of the fruitful woman,[16] because it takes place in the daytime, in the light which nothing temporal can enter. Everything that the sun ever shone on or that was touched by time never came to this light,[17] therefore the seed is receptive in this light.[18] In the light the seed is conceived, therefore the fruit is nobler, and there are far more sons, and not daughters,[19] for whatever might prevent the birth of sons[20] . . . therefore there are sons and there are many more sons, because it occurs above time, in the day.

The other reasons why there are more sons [is] because it occurs frequently in the day, indeed a hundred times and far more: as many more as the soul is able to conceive, so the birth takes place in the soul.[21] Therefore there are many more sons, because it occurs in the day, and frequently in the day, and at that time there are many sons. For it is in eternity that sons shall come to be. Over two thousand years ago she abandoned that in the school [?][22] which will happen in a thousand times a thousand years: over that eternity spreads itself. If a man were to have thirty children over a period of thirty years, and if he had everything that can happen to a man in a thousand years or in twenty thousand years — eternity plants that, which has become fruit and ripened,[23] and it becomes ripe in one moment. Therefore there are many sons, because it occurs in eternity at the. . . . [When] God gives Himself, He gives Himself altogether.[24] He either gives or does not give to the extent that the soul can receive, because God must needs pour Himself out all at once here[25] . . . burst, He would have burst if He had not poured Himself out all at once, for no creature existed into whom He could pour Himself out altogether, and therefore He begot a Son into whom He could pour Himself out altogether. Therefore there are sons . . . [in] eternity. A man who had great joy would not be silent about it. A master says, if anyone were with the sun and with the moon and saw the wonders there, if he could not tell anyone he could not endure it. He[26] said then: . . . "Cast out the maid and her son, for he shall not inherit with the freeborn children" (Gen. 21:10; Gal. 4:30). All corporeal prayer and fasting and all outward ways do not belong to the inheritance.[27] And after that all spiritual things that work in the spirit do not belong to the inheritance.[28] However great the desire, cast out the maid and her son, then one can gain a great and immeasurable reward from fasting and praying and spiritual works . . .[29]

Notes

1. MS 80 18537, Germanisches Nationalmuseum, Nürnberg, fragment discovered by Kurt Ruh in 1967: a double sheet from an old MS which had been subsequently used as a cover for documents, slightly trimmed at the edges and with four holes made by the later binder. Some words are illegible through friction. Written probably about 1300, and certainly not later than 1325 (thus during Eckhart's lifetime), perhaps by a female scribe. It is thus the oldest MS of any of Eckhart's sermons. Published in diplomatic reprint, with facsimile, in the *Zeitschrift für deutsches Altertum* 111 (1982), pp. 219–25. The following notes are based almost entirely on Professor Ruh's article, for which this general acknowledgement may suffice. My own contribution is negligible, apart from keying the textual references, instead of to DW, to the present translation. For reference

purposes I have numbered this as Sermon 98.

2. The word intended must be 'widow', which I have accordingly supplied in the text: cf. No. 79 (II, p. 229); see also No. 15 (I, p. 260), and *Talks of Instruction* 3.

3. Cf. No. 60 (II, p. 104), and No. 14b (I, pp. 127ff.).

4. Cf. Luke 8:11 and Augustine, *Enarratio in Ps. 84*, 15 (PL 37, 1079f.): 'Semen Dei in cordibus vestris'. See also *The Nobleman*, p. 107.

5. Cf. No. 10 (I, pp. 92f.).

6. Cf. No. 19 (I, p. 155).

7. Cf. No. 71 (II, p. 181).

8. Cf. especially No. 66 (II, p. 142); also No. 53 (II, p. 64) and No. 18 (I, pp. 147f.).

9. Cf. No. 20 (I, p. 165).

10. There is an obvious break in the sense here. Perhaps the scribe missed out a line in his (her?) copy, or it may be a case of homoteleuton (jumping from one passage to another with a similar ending): a frequent cause of scribal errors. In any case a 'first point' must have been made before the 'secondly'.

11. There is probably another omission here: the literal rendering is 'when the soul *does not* stand . . .', which makes little sense in the context.

12. *Redelichkeit*, as in No. 7 (I, p. 64). Cf. also No. 1, no. 9 (I, p. 13), where it is pointed out that this refers to the 'higher intellect', not the ratiocinative faculty.

13. Cf. No. 66 (II, pp. 142, 144).

14. Quotation untraced.

15. This 'he' has no grammatical reference, but Isaiah or St Paul must be meant: see next note.

16. Cf. Gal. 4:27 (quoting Isaiah 54. 1). Also mentioned but not discussed, LW I, 663.

17. Cf. No. 29 (I, p. 216).

18. Cf. No. 79 (II, p. 230).

19. Cf. No. 66 (II, p. 142).

20. Slightly obscure: there is probably something omitted. Ruh compares a passage from Pfeiffer No. 26 (the authenticity of which has not, so far, been confirmed): 'and if this nature were not prevented, a son would always be being born as with the heavenly Father' (transl. Evans I, p. 77). However, Quint 1932 emended the words 'as (with) the heavenly Father', on the basis of other manuscript evidence, to 'and never any daughter', which is slightly closer to the present text. Cf. No. 31 (I, p. 231), and No. 17 (I, p. 144).

21. Cf. No. 79 (II, p. 230), also No. 69 (II, p. 165).

22. This passage is hopelessly corrupt. 'She' probably refers to the soul, and the reference is obviously to the paradox of time and eternity.

23. Conjectural reading by Ruh.

24. Cf. No. 10 (I, p. 94).

25. Cf. No. 79 (II, p. 230). See also *On Detachment*, n. 2 and No. 73 (II, p. 197), also No. 48 (II, p. 33).

26. This should be 'she': the speaker is Sara. But cf. n. 15.

27. Cf. Rom. 8:17, Gal. 4:7; No. 40 (I, p. 285) and No. 66 (II, p. 143).

28. This sentence is hopelessly corrupt.

29. Josef Quint considered this text, as he wrote on 29 February 1972 to Kurt Ruh, to be 'pieced together from various borrowings or excerpts by a compiler with no understanding', whereas Ruh argues, and rightly as I think, that it is indeed part of a single sermon, however badly transmitted. The type of patchwork compilation Quint had in mind only came into existence after the mid-fourteenth century, whereas the palaeographical evidence proves beyond doubt that our manuscript is much earlier than this.

The gist of Ruh's analysis is as follows: Eckhart does not intend to expand here on the 'abandoning of creatures' (as indicated in the 'widow' simile), as he has frequently done this. He turns to the theme of 'a light in the soul', but quickly goes on to the parable of the sower (Matt. 13:24f.), linking this with the theme of light. The excursus on the heart being in the middle of the body is related by its connection to the birth of the Word in the soul, and then the 'light' theme is varied by reference to an unknown 'master' who declared that those born in the day are nobler than those born at night. The theme is related to Gal. 4:27, which brings us back to the widow mentioned in the beginning of our fragment. Ruh compares the treatment in No. 79. The remaining part can all be related to Gal. 4:27, and Ruh explains the apparent digression about a man's excessive joy by reference to the statement that God must of necessity pour Himself out into creatures. Despite the corruption of text towards the end, the theme of 'sons and heirs' is maintained logically (Ruh refers to Gal. 4:7 *quod si filius, et heres per Deum*, which the *New English Bible* renders: "and if a son, then also by God's own act an heir").

As regards the state of the text, Professor Ruh, in a letter of 7 December 1982, writes:

That is what — at best — texts looked like that were based on notes taken down without any help or correction from the author. The greatest part of the manuscript tradition of Eckhart is — fortunately for us! — not like this.

APPENDIX I
FOUR ECKHART LEGENDS
(Pf. III, 67–70, QT pp. 443–8)

1. *A Good Morning*[1]

Meister Eckhart said to a poor man, 'God give you good morning, brother.'

'Keep it for yourself, sir, I have never had a bad one.'

He said, 'How is that, brother?'

'Because whatever God has sent me to suffer, I have suffered gladly for His sake and have considered myself unworthy of Him, and so I have never been sad or troubled.'

He asked, 'Where did you first find God?'[2]

'When I left all creatures behind, then I found God.'

He said, 'Where did you leave God, brother?'

'In every pure, clean heart.'

He said, 'What kind of a man are you, brother?'

'I am a king.'

He asked, 'Of what?'

'Of my flesh: for whatever my spirit desired from God, my flesh was always more nimble and quick to perform and endure than my spirit was to receive.'

He said, 'A king must have a kingdom. What is your realm, brother?'

'In my soul.'

He said, 'In what way, brother?'

'When I have closed the doors of my five senses and desire God with all my heart, I find God in my soul, as radiant and joyous as He is eternal life.'

He said, 'You must be a saint. Who made you one, brother?'

137

'Sitting still and raising my thoughts aloft and uniting with God — that has drawn me up to heaven, for I could find no rest in anything that was less than God. Now I have found Him I have rest and joy in Him eternally, and that surpasses all temporal kingdoms. There is no outward work so perfect, but it hinders the inner life.'

2. *The Naked Boy*[3]

He said, 'I come from God.'

'Where did you leave Him?'

'In virtuous hearts.'

'Where are you going?'

'To God.'

'Where will you find Him?'

'Where I abandoned all creatures.'

'Who are you?'

'A king.'

'Where is your kingdom?'

'Mind that no one shares it with you.'

'I will.'

Then he took the boy into his cell and said, 'Take whichever coat you like.'

'Then I would not be a king!'[4] And he vanished.

It was God Himself having fun with him.

3. *Meister Eckhart's Daughter*[5,6]

A young girl[7] came to a Dominican convent and asked for Meister Eckhart. The porter said, 'Whom shall I announce?'

She replied, 'I don't know.'

He said, 'Why don't you know?'

She said, 'Because I am neither a girl nor a woman, nor

husband nor wife, nor widow nor virgin, nor master nor maid nor manservant.'

The porter went to Meister Eckhart. 'Come out to the strangest creature I ever saw, and let me go with you, and put your head out and ask: "Who wants me?" ' He did so. She spoke to him the same as she had spoken to the porter.

He said, 'My dear child, you speak truthfully and with a ready tongue: explain to me more fully what you mean.'

She said, 'If I were a girl, I would still be in my primal innocence; if I were a woman, I would be bearing the eternal Word without cease in my soul; if I were a man, I should put up a stiff resistance to all sins; if I were a wife, I should be faithful to my sole and beloved husband; if I were a widow, I should ever yearn for my one and only love; if I were a virgin, I should be in reverent service; if I were a master, I would command all the divine virtues; if I were a maid, I should be meekly subject to God and all creatures; if I were a manservant, I should be hard at work, serving my Lord with my whole will and without contradiction. But I am none of all these things: I am just a thing like anything else and go my way.'

The master went and said to his brothers, 'It seems to me that I have just heard the purest person I have ever met.'[8]

4. Meister Eckhart's Feast[9]

Once[10] a poor man came to Cologne on the Rhine in quest of poverty and the life of truth. Then a maiden came to him and said, 'Dear child, will you eat with me in God's love?'

'Gladly', he said.

When they sat down, she said, 'Eat heartily, don't be ashamed.'

'If I eat too much it is wrong, if I eat too little it is wrong. The middle way is best: I will eat like a poor man.'

She asked, 'What is a poor man?'

He said, 'That consists in three things. The first is that he is dead to all natural things. The second is that he cannot desire too much of God. The third is that he should desire whatever is termed, or is, suffering for no one more than for himself.'

She said, 'My dear child, tell me, what is the poverty of the inner man?'

He said, 'That too lies in three things. The first is utter detachment from all creatures, in time and in eternity. The second is determined humility of the inner and the outer man. The third is a diligent devotion and a continual raising of the mind to God.'

She said, 'Indeed, I am glad to hear that. Now, dear child, tell me, what is the poverty of the spirit?'

He said, 'You ask too much!'

She said, 'I never heard that there could be too much of what concerns God's glory and man's blessedness.'

The poor man said, 'You speak truly. This too consists in three things. The first is, that a man should know nothing in time or eternity but God alone. The second is, that he should not seek God outside of himself. The third is, that he should not carry any spiritual goods, as his personal property,[11] from place to place.'

'Well then, should not the Master, your father and mine, not carry his sermon from his cell to the pulpit?'

He replied, 'Not he.'

'Why?' she asked.

He said, 'The more temporal, the more physical; the more

physical, the more temporal.'[12]

She said, 'This spirit did not come from Bohemia!'

He said, 'The sun that shines on Cologne also shines on the city of Prague.'[13]

She said, 'Explain that to me more clearly.'

He said, 'It is not my place with the Master here present.'

The Master said, 'If a man has not the truth within, let him love it outside, then he will also find it within.'[14]

She said, 'This meal is well paid for.'

Then the poor man said, 'Maiden, now you must pay for the wine!'

'Gladly', she replied, 'just ask me.'

He asked, 'How can a man recognise the works of the Holy Ghost in his soul?'

She said, 'By three things. The first is that he daily grows less in the way of bodily things, desires and natural love. The second is that he continually grows in divine love and grace. The third is that, with love and eagerness, he devotes his labours more to his fellow men than to himself.'

He said, 'Our Lord's chosen friends have given good evidence of this.' Then he said, 'How can a spiritual man tell if God is present at his prayers and exercises?'

She said, 'By three things. The first is by the object which God sets before His chosen ones: that is the scorn of the world and physical suffering. The second is by a growth in grace commensurate with the love that is between him and God. The third is, that God never leaves that man without indicating some new path of wisdom to him.'

He said, 'That must indeed be true. Now tell me, how can a man tell if all his works are performed according to the sovran will of God?'

She said, 'By three things. The first is, that he never lacks a clear conscience. The second is, that he never turns from union with God. And the third is, that the heavenly Father begets His Son in him continually by grace.'

The Master said, 'If all debts were as well paid off as this wine, there is many a soul in purgatory that would now be in eternal life.'

Then the poor man said, 'If there is any more to pay, that is up to the Master.'

Then the Master said, 'Let old age be privileged.'

But the poor man said, 'Let love do its work, which knows no distinctions.'[15]

The maiden said, 'You are a Master whose skill has been proven three times in Paris.'

The poor man said, 'I would rather have someone who had been tried and proven once in the truth than three times in Paris in the chair.'

Meister Eckhart said, 'If there was anything that needed saying to me, it has been said.'[16]

The maiden said, 'Tell me, Father, how can anyone know he is a child of the heavenly Father?'

He said, 'By three things. The first is, that a man performs all his actions out of love. The second is, that he accepts all things equally from God. The third is, that he pins all his hopes on none but God alone.'

The poor man said, 'Tell me, Father, how can anyone know whether virtue is operative in him to the highest degree of nobility?'

He said, 'By three things: you must love God for God's sake, the good for good's sake, and the truth for truth's sake.'

The Master said, 'Dear children, how should he live who preaches the truth?'

The maiden said, 'He should so live that what he preaches in words, he practises with deeds.'

The poor man said, 'That is good. But he should be inwardly so established that he has more truth within him than he can put into outward words.[17] As the eternal Word is begotten of the heavenly Father, so the will of God is the begetting and becoming of all creatures.'[18]

This is Meister Eckhart's Feast.[19]

Notes

1. Pf. III, 67. The 'poor man' evidently represents the 'poor in spirit' so frequently mentioned by Eckhart.

2. Cf. *On Detachment*, third paragraph.

3. Pf. III, 68. A variant on the same theme as No. 1.

4. Perhaps derived from such texts as No. 63 (II, p. 118).

5. Pf. III, 69.

6. My own heading. Quint heads this, with the Munich and Wolfenbüttel MSS discovered by him, 'About a good sister: a goodly conversation she had with Meister Eckhart'. This piece seems to be developed (negatively turned and expanded) from the theme of the 'virgin who was a wife' referred to in No. 8 (I, pp. 71ff.).

7. The word used is 'daughter' (*tohter*), which can also mean 'young girl', 'pupil', or 'penitent' (modern German *Beichtkind*, lit. 'confession-child').

8. Pfeiffer's text, from a Stuttgart MS, concludes: 'This parable (*bîspel*) is called *Meister Eckhart's Daughter*' (cf. n. 6 above), which perhaps links it with the better-known 'Sister Cathy' (Pf. II, 6, transl. Evans I, pp. 312–334), the heading of which is 'This is Sister Cathy (*Swester Katrei*), Meister Eckhart's Daughter from Strassburg', an elaborate piece containing possible reminiscences of the present text, in which the 'daughter' finally declares that she has 'become God', and proceeds to instruct the Master. The text is later than Eckhart's time, but if such sentiments reached the ears of the Archbishop of Cologne, this would go far to explain his anxiety to have the Master's teachings condemned!

9. Pf. III, 70. Quint gives a full analysis of this text, which is found in a number of MSS (QT, pp. 529–531). I give the gist of the commentary here. Each of the

three partners in the discussion, the poor man, the maiden, and the Master, has to answer three questions, and each answer is itself in three parts. There are also two short 'intermissions' and a concluding section (see below).

10. Pfeiffer's text, followed by Evans, opens with the words 'Meister Eckhart said'. These words, which are not found in all MSS, are clearly wrong and are omitted by Quint.

11. Eckhart's word is *eigenschaft*, meaning something like 'ownness' or 'possessiveness': cf. No. 6 (I, p. 57 and n. 3 there).

12. Quint suggests that the carrying of the spiritual property of the preacher from his cell to the pulpit, being an act in time and space, drags the spiritual down to the material world. See n. 14, and n. 19 (end).

13. The 'poor man' is supposed to have come from Bohemia, of which province Eckhart had been made Vicar-General in 1307. From about 1322 Eckhart was in Cologne (see Introduction, Vol. I, pp. xix-xx). The maiden suggests that the spirit of the poor man's reply is that of Cologne (i.e of Eckhart), which he cannot have 'brought with him', in the sense referred to, from Prague. The poor man indicates by the image of the sunshine, that the same spirit is after all not unknown in Prague (Q). He also implies, I think, that in spiritual matters neither time (at least 15 years earlier) nor place is relevant; also, being 'poor in spirit', he has not carried it as his personal property, emphasising this by refusing to elaborate further in the presence of the Master himself.

14. Quint interprets this too as a response to the poor man's words about 'carrying his sermon from his cell to the pulpit', namely that anyone who does not find the truth within must learn to love it when he hears it preached (and that the preacher *must*, therefore, 'carry it to the pulpit'). If he loves what he hears, *then* he will indeed be able to find it within.

15. Since love knows no distinctions, age has no special privileges (Q).

16. This paragraph is missing in all but two MSS, in one of which it is misplaced (Q). Eckhart was in fact three times in Paris (1293, ca. 1300–02, and 1311–12) (cf. Introduction, Vol. I, xviii-xx), and certainly 'proved himself' in disputation there. But, says the poor man, to have been 'tried and proven' in the *truth* is more important than such academic distinctions. Despite its omission in several MSS, this passage is a necessary and important element in the dialogue. Its omission is ascribable merely to a scribal oversight (inefficiently 'corrected' in the Munich text) and not to any doctrinal misgivings.

17. Finally, the Master questions the maiden and the poor man, and the poor man's reply supplements that of the maiden. This indicates that he is wiser than she is, while the Master is, of course, wiser than both. Their answers together

indicate the relation that should exist between the teacher or preacher, and the truth that he declares (Q).

18. Quint omits these words, found in Pfeiffer's text. Their relevance is not perhaps immediately obvious, but they do point to the distinction between 'outward words' and the eternal Word. Even if they are genuine (which I think probable), it is not quite clear whether they form part of the poor man's speech or not. Cf. No. 36 (I, p. 266) and No. 22 (I, p. 179).

19. Quint has instead of this a doggerel verse from the Munich MS:

> This is Meister Eckhart's sermon and question.
> Whoever hears them or repeats them,
> May God grant him a goodly end
> And after this life a happy resurrection. Amen.

This is a typical scribe's verse, certainly not attributable to the author of the dialogue, and of no interest except for its expression of faith in the Master. It is certainly less relevant than the words mentioned above (n. 18). It is also inaccurate since the piece in question is not a 'sermon' of the Master's. On the other hand, the term 'feast' (*wirtschaft*) in Pfeiffer's text is in accordance with the contents; indeed, since wine is included we might even speak of a 'symposium'! Quint calls the whole an 'ovation' for Meister Eckhart and quotes with approval Friedrich von der Leyen's words (*Zeitschrift für deutsche Philologie* 38 (1906), p. 356) that it 'emanates from the circle of our Master's disciples', or that it was 'produced under his immediate influence'. We can, I think, go a little further. The dialogue clearly emanates from those who had known the Master in his last days in Cologne. It is rigidly disciplined in form and content, and shows accurate knowledge of the Master's life (e.g. his three visits to Paris, cf. n. 16, and his activity in Bohemia) as well as of his teachings. It is not merely an 'ovation' but a *defence* of the Master, whether produced before or after his death (cf. n. 8). In this connection, the poor man's avoidance of excess is significant: on being urged to eat heartily he says he will eat neither too much nor too little. This could be an implied criticism of some more intemperate followers of the Master, alluded to by Suso in Chapter 6 of his *Little Book of Eternal Wisdom* (transl. Clark, London 1953) in the shape of the 'nameless wild one' who, in the manner of some recent Western Zen enthusiasts, misinterpreted the Master's teachings as 'unrestrained liberty'.

There is another possible interpretation of the discussion (cf. nn. 12, 13, 14) about the Master's 'carrying his sermon from his cell to the pulpit', which the poor man deprecates and the Master justifies. As Eckhart himself had said in one sermon (No. 56 (II, p. 82)): 'Whoever has understood this sermon, good luck to

him. If no one had been here I should have had to preach it to this collecting-box.'
He *had* to preach of that which he knew, even in the full knowledge that he would
be misunderstood, and despite the realisation that he would probably be — as he
was — persecuted for it.

APPENDIX II
THE MASTER'S FINAL WORDS [1]
(Pf. p. 685f.)

Meister Eckhart was besought by his good friends, 'Give us something to remember, since you are going to leave us.'

He said, 'I will give you a rule, which is the keystone[2] of all that I have ever said, which comprises[3] all truth that can be spoken of or lived.

'It often happens that what seems trivial to us is greater in God's sight than what looms large in our eyes. Therefore we should accept all things equally from God, not ever looking and wondering which is greater, or higher, or better.[4] We should just follow where God points out for us, that is, what we are inclined to and to which we are most often directed, and where our bent is. If a man were to follow that path, God would give him the most in the least, and would not fail him.

'It often happens that people spurn the least, and thus they prevent themselves from getting the most in the least, which is wrong. God is in all modes, and equal in all modes, for him who can take Him equally.[5] People often wonder whether their inclinations come from God or not, and this is how to find out: if a man finds it within himself to be willing above all things to obey God's will in all things, provided he knew or recognised it, then he may know that whatever he is inclined to, or is most frequently directed to, is indeed from God.

'Some people want to find God as He shines before them, or as He tastes to them. They find the light and the taste, but they do not find God. A scripture declares that God shines in the darkness, where we sometimes least recognise Him.[6]

147

Where God shines least for us is often where He shines the most. Therefore we should accept God equally in all ways and in all things.

'Now someone might say, "I would take God equally in all ways and in all things, but my mind will not abide in this way or that, so much as in another." To that I say he is wrong. God is in all ways and equal in all ways, for anyone who can take Him so. If you get more of God in one way than in another, that is fine, but it is not the best. God is in all ways and equal in all ways, for anyone who can take Him so. If you take one way, such and such, that is not God. If you take *this* and *that*, you are not taking God, for God is in all ways and equal in all ways, for anyone who can take Him so.

'Now someone might say, "But if I do take God equally in all ways and in all things, do I not still need some special way?" Now see. In whatever way you find God most, and you are most often aware of Him, that is the way you should follow. But if another way presents itself, quite contrary to the first, and if, having abandoned the first way, you find God as much in the new way as in the one that you have left, then that is right. But the noblest and best thing would be this, if a man were come to such equality, with such calm and certainty that he could find God and enjoy Him in *any* way and in *all* things, without having to wait for anything or chase after anything: *that* would delight me![7] For this, and to this end all works are done, and every work helps towards this. If anything does not help towards this, you should let it go.

'We thank thee, heavenly Father, that thou hast given us thine only-begotten Son, in whom thou givest thyself and all things. We pray thee, heavenly Father, for the sake of thine only-begotten Son, our Lord Jesus Christ, through whom thou neither wilt nor canst deny anything to anyone — hear us in him, and make us free and bare of all our manifold faults and unite us, in him, with thee. Amen.'

Notes

1. My title. This piece is included, as if by an afterthought, on the final two pages of Pfeiffer. Quint 1932 treats it as 'sermon 111' and introduces some emendations, which I have adopted. Not included in Q or QT but translated by Miss Evans and, badly, by Blakney.

Whereas the four pieces translated in Part I of this Appendix can only be classed as entirely apocryphal, however spiritually profound or poetic we may find them, there is some possibility that this reflects, however indistinctly, a genuine tradition of what the Master may have said to his disciples before leaving for Avignon. It is after all entirely probable that he would have been asked for a 'last word', and that his parting message would have been lovingly preserved.

2. The word is *slôz* which, like modern German *Schloss*, can mean both 'castle' and 'lock', but in Middle High German it can also mean 'keystone'.

3. The verb used is *beslozzen* 'enclosed', which links it with *slôz*. The play on words (as in No. 66, II, p. 142 and n. 14 there) cannot be reproduced in English.

4. Cf. *Book of Divine Comfort* 6 and n. 7 there for further references.

5. This is repeated again and again in what follows with the hammer-blow effect of a Buddhist *sutta*. In many a sermon Eckhart has described the birth of the Word in the human soul and other mysteries. Here, in his final exhortation (if such it really is), he is insisting on what his disciples ought to *do*. It is above all the essence of his *practical* teaching. This, I think, lends weight to the argument in favour of the authenticity of this text.

6. This seems to be a paraphrase of John 1:5.

7. Blakney mistranslates (and italicises): '*this has been my joy!*' But Eckhart's *daz behagete mir* is subjunctive. Miss Evans's version is different but no better: 'a boon accorded to me'. Blakney is also wrong in declaring that the 'chief message' of this text was forbidden on the basis of two quotations (which seem to me of dubious relevance) from the defence documents. Since in any case the passages quoted were not condemned in the Bull of 1329, their sense cannot be said to have been 'forbidden'.

CONCORDANCES

W = the present translation; Pf. = Pfeiffer; E = Evans
(B = Vol. II); Q = Quint, DW; QT = Quint 1955;
B = Blakney; C = Clark 1957 (CS = Clark–Skinner
1958).

CONCORDANCE A

W	Pf.	E	Q	QT	B	C
			Vol. I			
1	1	1	—	57	1	—
2	2	2	—	58	2	—
3	3	3	—	—	3	—
4	4	4	—	59	4	—
5	5	5	65	—	—	—
6	6	6	1	1	13	—
7	7	7	76	35	—	1
8	8	8	2	2	24	2
9	9	B II 2	86	—	—	—
10	10	B II 11	25	38	17	3
11	11	11	26	49	—	—
12	12	12	27	50	—	—
13a	—	—	5a	5	—	22
13b	13	13	5b	6	5	—
14a	—	—	16a	—	—	—

CONCORDANCES

W	Pf.	E	Q	QT	B	C
14b	14	14	16b	—	—	4
15	15	—	—	44	8	—
16	74	74	29	29	21	—
17	81	81	28	31	20	—
18	66	66	30	43	—	CS p. 58
19	19	19	71	37	—	8
20	20	20	44	—	—	—
21	21	21	17	17	—	5
22	22	22	53	—	—	—
23	23	23	47	—	—	—
24a	—	—	13	14	—	23
24b	24	24	13a	15	—	—
25	25	25	3	3	9	6
26	—	B II 45	57	—	—	—
27	27	27	34	—	—	—
28	28	28	78	—	—	—
29	(29)	(29) / B II 27	38	—	—	—
30	30	30	45	—	—	—
31	31	31	37	—	—	—
32a	32	32	20a	20	—	7
32b	—	—	20b	21	—	—
33	33	33	35	—	—	—
34	34	—	55	—	—	—

CONCORDANCES

W	Pf.	E	Q	QT	B	C
35	35	35	19	19	—	—
36	36	36	18	18	7	—
37	37	37	—	—	—	—
38	38	38	36a	—	—	—
39	—	—	36b	—	—	—
40	40	40	4	4	19	10
41	41	41	70	53	—	—
42	42	42	69	—	15	11
Vol. II						
43	43	B III, 12	41	46	—	—
44	—	—	58	—	—	—
45	45	45	60	45	—	—
46	46	—	54b	—	—	—
47	47	47	46	—	—	—
48	48	48	31	47	—	—
49	49	49	77	—	—	—
50	—	—	14	—	—	25
51	—	—	15	—	—	24
52	—	—	32	30	14	—
53	88	88	22	23	—	18
54	—	—	23	—	—	—
55	55	55	62	48	—	—
56	56	56	—	26	27	12
57	96	96	12	13	—	—

CONCORDANCES

W	Pf.	E	Q	QT	B	C
58	58	B III, 13	66	27	—	—
59	59	59	39	25	—	CS 53
60	60	60	48	34	—	—
61	61	61	—	—	—	—
62	62	62	82	54	—	—
63	63	63	40	—	—	—
64	64	64	81	—	—	—
65	65	65	6	7	18	13
66	83	83	10	11	25	16
67	84	84	9	10	26	17
68	90	90	11	12	12	19
69	69	69	68	36	6	—
70	—	—	67	—	—	—
71	—	—	59	—	—	—
72	72	—	7	8	—	14
73	73	73	73	33	—	—
74	74	(86)	74	—	—	—
75	75	—	—	—	—	—
76	—	B III, 50	61	—	—	—
77	—	—	63	—	—	—
78	—	B III, 1	64	—	—	—
79	79	79	43	52	—	—
80	80	80	42	39	—	—
81	—	B III, 38	33	—	—	—

CONCORDANCES

W	Pf.	E	Q	QT	B	C
82	82	82	8	9	16	15
83	102	102	51	24	11	—
84	—	B III, 42	84	—	—	—
85	—	B III, 43	85	—	—	—
86	—	B III, 32	56	—	—	—
87	87	87	52	32	28	—
88	85	85	75	—	—	—
89	89	89 / B III, 14	49	—	—	—
90	103	103	—	—	—	—
91	91	91	79	41	10	—
92	94	94	24	—	—	—
93	95	95	50	—	—	—
94	97	97	80	55	—	—
95	98	98	72	56	—	—
96	99	99	83	42	23	—
97	100	100	21	22	—	21
			Vol. III			
I	II, 17	B II, 1	V, 3	p. 53	p. 3	CS p. 63
II	II, 5	II, 5 / B II, 2	V, 1	p. 101	p. 43	CS p. 109
III	—	B II, 2	V, 2	p. 140	p. 74	CS p. 149
IV	II, 9	II, 9	V, 4	—	p. 82	CS p. 160
V (=98)	—	—	—	—	—	—

154

CONCORDANCES

W	Pf.	E.	Q	QT	B	C
App. I, 1	III, 67	III, 67	—	p. 444	p. 251	—
2	III, 68	III, 68	—	p. 444	p. 252	—
3	III, 69	III, 69	—	p. 443	p. 252	—
4	III, 70	III, 70	—	p. 445	—	—
App. II	p. 684	p. 482	—	—	p. 256	—

CONCORDANCE B

Pf.		W	Q	QT	B	C
No. 1	p. 3	1	—	57	1	—
2	10	2	—	58	2	—
3	16	3	—	—	3	—
4	24	4	—	59	4	—
5	30	5	65	—	—	—
6	33	6	1	1	13	—
7	38	7	76	35	—	1
8	42	8	2	2	24	2
9	47	9	86	28	—	—
10	54	10	25	38	17	3
11	57	11	26	49	—	—
12	60	12	27	50	—	—
13	64	13b	5b	6	5	—
14	67	14b	16b	16	—	4

CONCORDANCES

Pf.		W	Q	QT	B	C
15	71	15	—	44	8	—
19	79	19	71	37	—	8
20	85	20	44	—	—	—
21	88	21	17	17	—	5
22	91	22	53	—	—	—
23	93	23	47	—	—	—
24	96	24b	13a	—	—	—
25	97	25	3	3	9	6
27	101	27	34	—	—	—
28	103	28	78	—	—	—
29	104	29	38	—	—	—
30	106	30	45	—	—	—
31	109	31	37	51	—	—
32	111	32a	20a	20	—	—
33	115	33	35	—	—	—
34	117	34	55	—	—	—
35	120	35	19	19	—	—
36	123	36	18	18	7	—
37	126	37	—	—	—	—
38	129	38	36a	—	—	—
40	134	40	4	4	19	10
41	138	41	70	53	—	—
42	140	42	69	40	15	11
43	145	43	41	46	—	—

CONCORDANCES

Pf.		W	Q	QT	B	C
45	152	45	60	45	—	—
46	154	46	54b	—	—	—
47	157	47	46	—	—	—
48	159	48	31	47	—	—
49	161	49	77	—	—	—
52	170	52	32	30	14	—
55	176	55	62	48	—	—
56	179	56	—	26	27	12
58	184	58	66	27	—	—
59	189	59	39	25	—	CS 53
60	192	60	48	34	—	—
61	194	61	—	—	—	—
62	195	62	82	54	—	—
63	197	63	40	—	—	—
64	200	64	81	—	—	—
65	202	65	6	7	18	13
66	206	18	30	43	—	CS 58
69	220	69	68	36	6	—
72	226	72	7	8	—	14
73	228	73	73	33	—	—
74	231	16	29	29	—	—
75	235	75	—	—	—	—
79	253	79	43	52	—	—
80	256	80	42	39	—	—

CONCORDANCES

Pf.		W	Q	QT	B	C
81	258	17	28	31	20	—
82	261	82	8	9	16	15
83	264	66	10	11	25	16
84	267	67	9	10	26	17
85	272	88	75	—	—	—
86	275	74	74	—	—	—
87	280	87	52	32	28	—
88	284	53	23	23	—	18
89	288	89	49	—	—	—
90	295	68	11	12	12	19
91	299	91	79	41	10	—
94	305	92	24	—	—	—
95	307	93	50	—	—	—
96	309	57	12	13	—	—
97	312	94	80	55	—	—
98	314	95	72	56	—	—
99	317	96	83	42	23	—
100	320	97	21	22	—	21
102	331	83	51	24	11	—

CONCORDANCE C

Q	(DW)	W	Pf.	Q	(DW)	W	Pf.
1	I, 3	6	6	3	46	25	25
2	21	8	8	4	58	40	40

CONCORDANCES

Q	(DW)	W	Pf.	Q	(DW)	W	Pf.
5a	75	13a	—	26	23	11	11
5b	83	13b	13	27	40	12	12
6	97	65	65	28	58	17	81
7	116	72	72	29	73	16	74
8	125	82	82	30	93	18	66
9	138	67	84	31	114	48	48
10	159	66	83	32	132	52	—
11	175	68	90	33	150	81	—
12	190	57	96	34	160	27	27
13	207	24a	—	35	173	33	33
13a	223	24b	24	36a	186	38	38
14	230	50	—	36b	198	39	—
15	244	51	—	37	210	31	31
16a	257	14a	—	38	227	29	29
16b	261	14b	14	39	251	59	59
17	279	21	21	40	272	63	63
18	294	36	36	41	285	43	43
19	308	35	35	42	301	80	80
20a	322	32a	32	43	316	79	79
20b	340	32b	—	44	336	20	20
21	353	97	100	45	360	30	30
22	371	53	88	46	378	47	47
23	393	54	—	47	394	23	23
24	414	92	94	48	413	60	60
25	II, 6	10	10	49	427	89	89

CONCORDANCES

Q	(DW)	W	Pf.	Q	(DW)	W	Pf.
50	454	93	95	73	259	73	73
51	464	83	102	74	274	73	86
52	486	87	87	75	292	88	85
53	528	22	22	76	310	7	7
54a	548	—	—	77	334	49	49
54b	564	46	46	78	351	28	28
55	575	34	34	79	363	91	91
56	588	86	—	80	378	94	97
57	594	26	—	81	395	64	64
58	610	44	—	82	422	62	62
59	623	71	—	83	437	96	99
60	III, 10	45	45	84	454	84	—
61	35	76	—	85	468	85	—
62	56	55	55	86	481	9	9
63	74	77	—				
64	86	78	—				
65	95	5	5				

Not in Q

Q	(DW)	W	Pf.	QT	W	Pf.	
66	108	58	58				
67	129	70	—				
68	140	69	69	26	56	56	
69	159	42	42	44	15	15	
70	187	41	41	57	1	1	
71	211	19	19	58	2	2	
72	239	95	98	59	4	4	

BIBLICAL INDEX

Numbers 1–97 refer to Sermons (Vols. I–II). II App. 38–45 refers to Appendix to Vol. II. In Vol. III, TI = *Talks of Instruction* (numbers refer to §§); BDC = *Book of Divine Comfort*, N = *The Nobleman*, D = *On Detachment* (numbers refer to pages). No. 98 refers to the Fragment of an Unknown Sermon (pp. 131ff.)

161